✍ **W9-DGY-014**

Illegal Drugs

Other Books in the Current Controversies Series:

Illegal Drugs

David Bender, *Publisher*
Bruno Leone, *Executive Editor*

Brenda Stalcup, *Managing Editor*
Scott Barbour, *Senior Editor*

Charles P. Cozic, *Book Editor*

CURRENT CONTROVERSIES

Cover photo: Tony Savino/Sipa Press

Library of Congress Cataloging-in-Publication Data

Illegal drugs / Charles P. Cozic, book editor.
    p. cm. — (Current controversies)
    Includes bibliographical references and index.
    ISBN 1-56510-683-0 (lib. bdg. : alk. paper). — ISBN 1-56510-682-2 (pbk. : alk. paper)
    1. Drug abuse—United States. 2. Drug legalization—United States. 3. Drug testing—United States. 4. Drug abuse—United States—Prevention. I. Cozic, Charles P., 1957–   . II. Series.
HV5825.I49   1998
364.1'77'0973—dc21   97-29281
                                                                       CIP

© 1998 by Greenhaven Press, Inc., PO Box 289009, San Diego, CA 92198-9009
Printed in the U.S.A.

Contents

Chapter 1: Is There a Drug Abuse Crisis?

Yes: There Is a Drug Abuse Crisis

No: There Is No Drug Abuse Crisis

have argued. In fact, current rates of adolescent marijuana use are actually well below rates from the 1970s. Moreover, no reliable data exists to support the argument that teenagers are starting to smoke marijuana at a younger age.

Chapter 2: Should Drug Testing Be Allowed?

Yes: Drug Testing Should Be Allowed

No: Drug Testing Should Not Be Allowed

Chapter 3: Are Antidrug Programs Effective?

Yes: Antidrug Programs Are Effective

No: Antidrug Programs Are Ineffective

Chapter 4: Should Illegal Drugs Be Legalized?

Yes: Illegal Drugs Should Be Legalized

No: Illegal Drugs Should Not Be Legalized

to an increase in violent crimes such as assault and murder. Drug legalization also would likely produce more physical illnesses and psychiatric problems among drug users and their family members.

Legalizing drugs would reverse the substantial decrease in the number of drug users since 1979. Drug legalization could double or triple the number of American adults and youths who have access to drugs.

Support for legalizing drugs is based on several faulty arguments. For example, proponents claim that eliminating drug laws would result in reduced crime; in fact, legalization would lead to increased drug use, which in turn would lead to a rise in violent crimes. In addition, advocates argue that legalization has been successful in European countries, but several European nations' attempts at drug legalization have failed and have been abandoned.

Foreword

By definition, controversies are "discussions of questions in which opposing opinions clash" (Webster's Twentieth Century Dictionary Unabridged). Few would deny that controversies are a pervasive part of the human condition and exist on virtually every level of human enterprise. Controversies transpire between individuals and among groups, within nations and between nations. Controversies supply the grist necessary for progress by providing challenges and challengers to the status quo. They also create atmospheres where strife and warfare can flourish. A world without controversies would be a peaceful world; but it also would be, by and large, static and prosaic.

The Series' Purpose

The purpose of the Current Controversies series is to explore many of the social, political, and economic controversies dominating the national and international scenes today. Titles selected for inclusion in the series are highly focused and specific. For example, from the larger category of criminal justice, Current Controversies deals with specific topics such as police brutality, gun control, white collar crime, and others. The debates in Current Controversies also are presented in a useful, timeless fashion. Articles and book excerpts included in each title are selected if they contribute valuable, long-range ideas to the overall debate. And wherever possible, current information is enhanced with historical documents and other relevant materials. Thus, while individual titles are current in focus, every effort is made to ensure that they will not become quickly outdated. Books in the Current Controversies series will remain important resources for librarians, teachers, and students for many years.

In addition to keeping the titles focused and specific, great care is taken in the editorial format of each book in the series. Book introductions and chapter prefaces are offered to provide background material for readers. Chapters are organized around several key questions that are answered with diverse opinions representing all points on the political spectrum. Materials in each chapter include opinions in which authors clearly disagree as well as alternative opinions in which authors may agree on a broader issue but disagree on the possible solutions. In this way, the content of each volume in Current Controversies mirrors the mosaic of opinions encountered in society. Readers will quickly realize that there are many viable answers to these complex issues. By questioning each author's conclusions, students and casual readers can begin to develop the critical thinking skills so important to evaluating opinionated material.

Current Controversies is also ideal for controlled research. Each anthology in the series is composed of primary sources taken from a wide gamut of informational categories including periodicals, newspapers, books, United States and foreign government documents, and the publications of private and public organizations. Readers will find factual support for reports, debates, and research papers covering all areas of important issues. In addition, an annotated table of contents, an index, a book and periodical bibliography, and a list of organizations to contact are included in each book to expedite further research.

Perhaps more than ever before in history, people are confronted with diverse and contradictory information. During the Persian Gulf War, for example, the public was not only treated to minute-to-minute coverage of the war, it was also inundated with critiques of the coverage and countless analyses of the factors motivating U.S. involvement. Being able to sort through the plethora of opinions accompanying today's major issues, and to draw one's own conclusions, can be a complicated and frustrating struggle. It is the editors' hope that Current Controversies will help readers with this struggle.

Greenhaven Press anthologies primarily consist of previously published material taken from a variety of sources, including periodicals, books, scholarly journals, newspapers, government documents, and position papers from private and public organizations. These original sources are often edited for length and to ensure their accessibility for a young adult audience. The anthology editors also change the original titles of these works in order to clearly present the main thesis of each viewpoint and to explicitly indicate the opinion presented in the viewpoint. These alterations are made in consideration of both the reading and comprehension levels of a young adult audience. Every effort is made to ensure that Greenhaven Press accurately reflects the original intent of the authors included in this anthology.

"While some observers advocate increased law enforcement efforts to seize drugs and uncover supply routes, others argue that more emphasis on drug treatment and prevention programs is necessary to reduce the demand for illegal drugs."

Introduction

America's "war on drugs" has cost billions of dollars annually since the early 1980s. For example, the federal government was projected to spend $16 billion to control illegal drugs in 1998, a nearly sixfold increase from the amount spent in 1985. The nation's antidrug campaign—including arrests of drug users and traffickers as well as the interdiction of drug shipments—has had mixed success. It helped to slash the number of regular users of illicit drugs from twenty-three million in 1981 to twelve million in 1996. Cocaine use, for example, has substantially declined. However, marijuana use among teenagers and the number of teen drug users doubled between 1992 and 1995.

Experts sharply disagree as to which strategies are most effective at reducing drug use in America, a country that surpasses all other nations in demand for illegal drugs. While some observers advocate increased law enforcement efforts to seize drugs and uncover supply routes, others argue that more emphasis on drug treatment and prevention programs is necessary to reduce the demand for illegal drugs.

Many politicians and others assert that law enforcement authorities, attacking each link from cultivation to street sales, have achieved significant reductions in supplies of illegal drugs. According to narcotics expert William J. Olson, "The record of prohibition is impressive." He notes that from 1982 to 1992, drug prohibition and interdiction reduced teenage drug use to its lowest level in twenty years, cut monthly cocaine use by 78 percent, and resulted in the seizure of nearly half of the cocaine produced worldwide. According to *New York Times* columnist A.M. Rosenthal, "The drug war has made substantial progress that would have been impossible without laws and public support."

As part of its drug control strategy, the U.S. Office of National Drug Control Policy (ONDCP) stresses the importance of cracking down on domestic and foreign sources of illegal drugs as well as seizing drugs at the nation's borders. The office's 1997 annual report states, "Opposing international criminal organizations that traffic in drugs at all stages of their operation and in all their operating environments is essential."

However, opponents of this strategy argue that it is futile to try to block the flow of illegal drugs into the United States. Critics of a supply-oriented approach concur with former San Jose, California, police chief Joseph McNamara, who says that this tactic is ineffective, counterproductive, and much like "throwing sand against the tide." Even if the supply of incoming drugs were effectively cut, these critics maintain, the production of domestic drugs such as marijuana and methamphetamine would increase to meet America's high demand.

Many observers propose that instead of concentrating on interdiction and prohibition, funding should be increased for drug education programs, such as the school-based D.A.R.E. (Drug Abuse Resistance Education), Life Skills Training, and similar curricula. Taught in most schools to children in kindergarten through high school, these programs stress the dangers associated with illegal drug use. According to advocates, drug awareness and education programs deserve much of the credit for the sharp drop in the overall use of illegal drugs since the early 1980s. Citing marked reductions in Americans' use of alcohol and tobacco due to improved awareness and education, sociologist William J. Chambliss writes, "The most effective way to reduce [drug] consumption is through education."

Other observers contend that effective drug treatment programs are more successful at reducing drug use than are interdiction and law enforcement efforts. According to a RAND Corporation study, "Treatment is seven times more cost-effective in reducing cocaine consumption than the best supply-control program." Drug treatment proponents assert that placement in an inpatient addiction program averages $15,000 per year, compared to the $30,000 cost of incarcerating a convicted drug user. Indeed, some states have passed laws that mandate drug treatment instead of imprisonment for nonviolent offenders.

Despite antidrug efforts, millions of Americans continue to use and abuse illegal drugs. According to the ONDCP, "We will have to apply ourselves with a resolve marked by continuing education for our citizens, the determination to resist criminals who traffic in illegal drugs, and the patience and compassion to treat individuals caught in the grip of illegal drugs." How best to reduce the consumption of drugs is one of the issues examined in *Illegal Drugs: Current Controversies*, in which authors debate the impact of drugs on society and America's response to the problem of drug abuse.

Chapter 1

Is There a Drug Abuse Crisis?

Chapter Preface

In 1996, a U.S. Department of Health and Human Services (HHS) drug-use survey found that approximately 11 percent of teenagers reported using drugs (primarily marijuana) the previous month, more than double the number from a survey taken four years earlier. During his 1996 presidential campaign, former U.S. senator Bob Dole called this trend "nothing short of a national tragedy," prompting much analysis of the severity of American teenagers' drug use.

Many observers agree with Dole's assessment. Citing a 1996 University of Michigan survey of teenage drug use, the *Wall Street Journal* stated, "The fact [is] that one-quarter of our 13-year-olds now do drugs." Some researchers warn that compared with just a few years ago, youths are more tolerant of illegal drugs, want to experiment with more potent substances, and know of more peers who have tried drugs. In the words of HHS secretary Donna E. Shalala, "Increasing numbers are reaching for drugs and risking their futures. We have a generation at risk."

However, other evidence suggests that the teen drug problem may not be so alarming. In an October 1996 radio address, Bill Clinton remarked, "All the evidence is that 90 percent of our children are drug free. They are doing the right thing. They are not experimenting." *Christian Science Monitor* writer Warren Richey adds, "Drug use by teens remains below the record levels of the late 1970s. In 1979, government statistics show, 16.3 percent of teens acknowledged using drugs." Furthermore, the University of Michigan survey found that although teenagers' use of marijuana had doubled since 1992, their use of hard drugs was rare. Only 2 percent of twelfth graders were current cocaine users, 2.5 percent had tried LSD the previous month, and just 1 percent had used heroin in the past year, according to the report.

In the following chapter, the authors examine the use of illegal drugs among youths as they debate whether America suffers from a drug abuse crisis.

More Children Are Using Drugs

by Partnership for a Drug-Free America

About the author: *Partnership for a Drug-Free America is a drug prevention organization in New York City.*

More 9- to 12-year-olds are using drugs and more are growing increasingly tolerant toward drug use, according to a study released March 4, 1997, by the Partnership for a Drug-Free America (PDFA). The study reveals that these children—who are just in the 4th, 5th and 6th grades—are receiving significantly less information about the dangers of drugs.

"Our new national research reveals for the first time that younger children are emulating the attitudes and behavior of their older peers, only at the worst possible time," said Richard D. Bonnette, president and CEO of the Partnership. "This is particularly significant because these children—most of whom don't use drugs now—are seeing fewer risks in drugs just as they're about to move from elementary school to junior high or middle school—where, according to the data, drug experimentation rates skyrocket."

Fewer Children View Drugs as Dangerous

The 1996 Partnership Attitude Tracking Study (PATS) found significant erosions in anti-drug attitudes and more 9- to 12-year-olds using illicit drugs, particularly marijuana. The study of 12,292 children, teens and parents shows that today's 4th, 5th and 6th graders are less likely to consider drugs harmful and risky; more likely to believe drug use is widespread and acceptable; more report having friends who use illicit drugs; and fewer report receiving information about the dangers of drugs from a variety of different sources.

"These findings are deeply disturbing, especially when you consider the age of these children," Bonnette said. "We know, through our research, that attitudes shape behavior. So it's no shock that the normalization of illicit drugs that has occurred among teenagers is now trickling down to younger children. With children less resistant to drugs as they leave the relative safety of elementary

From Partnership for a Drug-Free America, "New National Study Finds More Children Using Drugs, Seeing Fewer Risks," press release, March 4, 1997, at www.drugfreeamerica.org/pats.html. Reprinted with permission.

school—and enter middle school, where their peers are older and drugs are much more a reality—the implications for the future are not encouraging."

The Partnership's Attitude Tracking Study is the largest on-going body of research on drug-related attitudes in America, funded, in large part, by a major organizational grant from the Robert Wood Johnson Foundation. It is the only national study to gather data on drug use and drug-related attitudes among children.

> *"The normalization of illicit drugs that has occurred among teenagers is now trickling down to younger children."*

This nationally-projectable study, now in its 9th installment, was conducted for PDFA by Audits & Surveys Worldwide Inc., a leading market research corporation based in New York.

Susceptibility to Drug Abuse Increases

Key Findings: 9- to 12-Year-Olds.

• One in four children was offered drugs during 1996 (24 percent of 9- to 12-year-olds in 1996, as compared with 19 percent in 1993). White children report an older friend or peer as the source for drugs; African-American and Hispanic children are also more likely to name "dealers" as their source;

• Trial use of marijuana increased among children from 2 to 4 percent—a statistically significant change, or an increase from approximately 230,000 children experimenting with the drug in 1995 to 460,000 children in 1996;

• Perceptions of peer drug use: The number of 11- to 12-year-olds who report having friends using marijuana increased from 7 to 13 percent between '93 and '96;

• Children are receiving less information about the dangers of drugs from a variety of different sources, especially mass media.

Table 1. Children were asked: "Did you learn a lot about the dangers of drugs from":

	1993	1996	Proportional Difference
School	79%	72%	–9%
TV shows, news, movies	53%	44%	–17%
TV commercials	50%	42%	–16%
Friends	43%	40%	–7%

"Children today spend about as many hours in front of a television as they do in a classroom," Bonnette said. "Clearly, children are learning less about the dangers of drugs from mass media, which is no surprise. There are fewer story-lines dealing with drugs on television, fewer anti-drug ads airing regularly, fewer stories about drugs. As the data demonstrate, when it comes to children and drugs, out of sight is out of mind."

• Less social disapproval of drugs: Children are less likely to believe that "people on drugs act stupid" (71 percent in 1995 to 65 percent in 1996); children are significantly less likely to say that they "don't want to hang around people who use drugs" (81 percent in 1993 to 75 percent in 1996);

• White children are showing more tolerance toward drugs. White children who agreed with the statement "Everybody tries drugs" went up from 21 percent in 1995 to 28 percent in 1996 (African-American children: 36 percent in 1995 to 28 percent in 1996);

• Fewer children report knowing what to do if someone offers them drugs.

Table 2. Children were asked what they'd do if someone they knew offered them drugs:

	1995	1996	Proportional Difference
Tell Mom or Dad	63%	55%	−13%
Tell the police	42%	36%	−14%
Tell a teacher	36%	29%	−19%
Tell the person not to use drugs	32%	25%	−22%

New Friends and Pressures

New Friends, New Pressures, New Peer and Social Norms. The study also found that the number of children who report experimenting with marijuana increases dramatically from 6th grade, where children remain in the relative safety of elementary school, to junior high or middle school, where children are exposed to a variety of new social and peer norms. The study found that 8 percent of 6th graders had experimented with marijuana, but 23 percent of 7th graders and 33 percent of 8th graders reported trying the drug.

"Parents and guardians need to know that if children aren't equipped with the right attitudes about drugs when they enter this grade and age, children will be more inclined to try drugs," Bonnette said. "Children are exposed to new friends, new pressures and new peer and social norms when they move into junior high. It is a totally new environment, where children will do almost anything—including drugs—to fit in."

> *"The number of children who report experimenting with marijuana increases dramatically from 6th grade . . . to junior high or middle school."*

Children continue to cite parents as a reliable source of information about the dangers of drugs—in 1993 and 1996, 67 percent of children named parents as a source. But, according to the study, parents of younger children are less inclined than parents of teenagers to talk with their children regularly about drugs: 42 percent of parents reported talking

18

to their teens on a regular basis, yet only 29 percent of parents with 9- to 12-year-olds reported discussing drugs with their children. And when they did, parents were more likely to talk generally about drugs versus specific drugs (marijuana, cocaine, etc.) and risks.

"From years of research, we know that regular communication with children about drugs is one of the most effective ways to reduce drug involvement among children," Bonnette said. "But too many adults believe 'it can't happen to my kid,' too few realize the risks kids face as they enter junior high. Parents can effectively safeguard their children from drugs, but they must start early, when children are in elementary school, and repeat the message often—particularly through the middle school years. Critical to keeping kids off drugs is frequent communication, which involves talking and listening—carefully listening to what kids know and feel about drugs."

Teens and Parents

Teens. As reported in other national studies, the Partnership's study found more teenagers using drugs in 1996. While some increases in drug use and some erosions in attitudes about the risks of drugs stabilized between 1995 and 1996, the data for teens show that use is still high, and attitudes weak, especially when compared with 1993 figures. The 1996 data indicate that most of the increases in drug use come from middle- and upper-income teens, and that their attitudes about drugs are much more lax than lower-income peers.

Parents and Teens. Today's parents—Baby Boomers, many of whom have used drugs—don't want their children using drugs, according to the Partnership's study. Although theories about Boomers' attitudes about drug use have been reported in the press, PATS demonstrates no evidence that parents today are tolerant of marijuana use among their children, despite past drug use among some parents. Instead, the problems facing parents today are the same ones as in the past—most parents continue to underestimate the prevalence of drugs in their children's lives, and most don't believe their children would ever get involved with drugs.

The Youth Drug Problem Is Greater than Reported

by National Center on Addiction and Substance Abuse

About the author: *The National Center on Addiction and Substance Abuse is a research group at Columbia University in New York City.*

In 1995, the National Center on Addiction and Substance Abuse at Columbia University (CASA) launched an annual survey on public attitudes toward illegal drugs and substance abuse (see our "National Survey of American Attitudes on Substance Abuse," July 1995). This study yielded unique insights into our national crisis of substance abuse. Far and away the most interesting and important results came from a modest subsample of teenagers, 12–17, included in that original survey essentially as an afterthought.

In 1996, we continued our investigation into those factors which contribute to a teenager's risk of substance abuse. Our focus on the situation of teenagers derives from the CASA thesis, substantiated by our other research, that addiction to drugs and other sorts of substance abuse typically has its roots in adolescence. Put alternatively, if we can get a kid through age 21 free of substance abuse, we are essentially home free.

A Same-Household Survey

In 1996, we expanded the sample of teens to 1200, and conducted the first study ever (to our knowledge) of parents and teenagers in the same household regarding their attitudes on drugs, alcohol and cigarettes. Of the 1200 teenagers we interviewed, and 1166 parents of teenagers, 1638 interviews were conducted in two-interview households (819 teens, 819 parents). This survey construction allows us to look at the characteristics, attitudes, and behaviors of the parents in our search for those risk factors which make a teen vulnerable to substance abuse.

Here are the "headlines" which emerge from our analysis:

• *Drugs still number one problem facing teens, say teens and parents.* Illegal drugs remain the most serious problem our teenagers face—in their own esti-

From National Center on Addiction and Substance Abuse, "Summary of Conclusions," in *National Survey of American Attitudes and Substance Abuse II*, September 1996, at www.casacolumbia.org/pubs/sep96/summary.htm. Reprinted with permission.

mation, as well as that of their parents.

• *It's worse than we realize.* The percentage of teenagers who say it is likely they will try an illegal drug in the future is 22%—twice the 11% we found in 1995.

This CASA study follows by less than a month the release of the 1995 National Household Study of Drug Abuse, which received a lot of attention for its report of the increase in drug use among teens. Our survey does not, like the National Household Study, ask teens directly if they use illegal drugs. But based on responses to other "indicator" questions, we find the extent of the substance abuse problem to be much greater than reported. By the time teenagers reach age 17, they are surrounded by illegal drugs in their schools, in their neighborhoods, and among their friends.

> *"The percentage of teenagers who say it is likely they will try an illegal drug in the future is 22%—twice the 11% we found in 1995."*

Ominous Statistics

Consider these facts. By the time teenagers reach 17:

• 68% can buy marijuana within a day;
• 62% have friends who use marijuana; 22% will say more than half of their friends use marijuana;
• 58% have been solicited to buy marijuana, 60% of boys, 57% of girls;
• 58% know someone who uses acid, cocaine, or heroin;
• 43% have a friend with a serious drug problem; 28% have more than one such friend;
• 42% find marijuana easier to buy than either beer or cigarettes;
• 79% have friends who smoke;
• 79% have friends who are regular drinkers; 34% know someone with a serious drinking problem (notice the incidence of serious drug problems is greater than serious drinking problems);
• 40% have witnessed the sale of drugs in their neighborhood;
• Less than 1 in 3 attend a drug-free school;
• Only 1 in 3 are willing to report a drug user or seller in their school to school officials.

• *Don't expect a teen to escape adolescence unscathed.* By the time a teen reaches 17, at best 12% can be categorized as least at-risk of substance abuse, according to the CASA index of risk for substance abuse, which is based upon a teen's proximity to illegal drugs and self-described likelihood of using drugs. The threat and temptation of illegal drugs, cigarettes, and alcohol have become near universal experiences for our nation's teens.

• *Your teen's school is probably not drug-free.* Most teens do not attend drug-free schools—indeed, for 1 in 8 teens, their schools are not even physically safe. Yet a plurality of parents blame "society at large" or others for this condition—instead of taking upon themselves the responsibility of demanding that our schools be made drug-free. Creating authentically drug-free schools—which our focus group research (and common sense) strongly suggests can only be accomplished by enrolling the students themselves in the project—is essential to the success of the fight for our kids.

Parents' Direct Experience

↓ • *Parents also touched by drugs.* The "drug culture" is not confined to the kids—a substantial number of parents of teenagers have the direct experience of illegal drugs in their daily lives as well:
  • 46% know someone who uses illegal drugs;
  • 32% have friends who use marijuana;
  • 19% have witnessed drugs being sold in their communities;
  • 49% of these "boomer" parents tried marijuana in their youth; 21% used it regularly.

Many baby-boom generation parents experimented with drugs, principally marijuana, during the 1960's and 70's. Those parents who used marijuana and whose teens know they used marijuana have teens at much higher risk of drug use than

> *"The threat and temptation of illegal drugs, cigarettes, and alcohol have become near universal experiences for our nation's teens."*

other teens. This, we think, illustrates what happens when there is parental ambivalence about the use of marijuana, the absence of a clear message that marijuana use is wrong.

The Threshold Age

• *Age 15 is the critical threshold.* As teens age, their proximity to drugs increases and their antipathy to drugs decreases. Drugs become perceived to be more benign, less of a "big deal"; they are ubiquitous, easier to get; there is less fear of using drugs, and such behavior comes to be regarded as "normal."

These changes occur continuously from ages 12 to 17, increasing the teen's risk of drug and substance abuse the older he or she gets. But there is a clear difference in the data between the pattern of responses of those 14 and under, and those 15 and older. This is the threshold age—roughly coinciding with the start of high school—at which all the risk indicators take a jump.

One implication of this finding is that we have to talk to teens of different ages in different ways. This may seem like an obvious point, but the decision to use illegal drugs will probably be made between ages 15–17, and discouraging drug use at these ages is a very different task from trying to inoculate a 12-year-old. Further, there is no reason provided by our data to be sanguine about the power of a broad drug inoculation strategy aimed at younger kids. There is no silver bullet here: fighting drug use is street warfare, requiring constant vigilance and activism.

Parental Awareness and Responsibility

• *Most parents know the score, are aware when their kids are at risk.* Parents do not suffer from naivete. Quite the opposite, it is impressive how realistic parents are regarding their teens' propensity to use drugs. Fully 46% say it is likely their teens will use illegal drugs—sadly, they appear to be right, based on the CASA index of risk of substance abuse.

• *But many parents figuratively toss in the towel.* A large number of parents (40%) think they have little influence over their adolescent's decision whether to use drugs or not. Many parents blame factors outside the family—friends of the teen or society at large—for a kid's use of illegal drugs, rather than the kid or the parent themselves.

The least at-risk teens are those whose parents say, as an example, that parents are responsible for the schools not being drug-free; the most at-risk teens are those whose parents say "society at large" is responsible for drugs in school. The extent to which a parent shoulders responsibility for their teen resisting drugs is a key factor in lowering in a teen's substance abuse risk score.

• *Controls on the sale of beer and alcohol work; cigarette restrictions are hollow.* All of our data yells at us: minors' access to alcohol and illegal drugs influences the extent of use.

CASA has set out the statistical relationships among smoking cigarettes, drinking alcohol, using marijuana, and serious drug addiction. The path to addiction typically begins with smoking cigarettes and drinking alcohol, leads to marijuana, and then on to serious drug use. No step on this path is inevitable, but this "gateway" principle makes clear that the best way to end new addictions among the young is by drawing a line on the abstinence side of marijuana use, underage smoking and drinking.

Our experience with controls on the sale of alcohol to minors proves we can make it harder for teens to buy cigarettes. For teens of all ages, beer and alcohol are consistently harder to buy than cigarettes. Teens are walking into stores which don't ask for ID's and purchasing smokes over the counter. If we are to take seriously the mission of denying cigarettes to teens,

> *"The decision to use illegal drugs will probably be made between ages 15–17."*

we must get serious about enforcing current restrictions on the sale of cigarettes to minors. It will not be sufficient but it is necessary.

• *Household products complicate our anti-drug task.* Almost every parent (92%) and almost as many teens (87%) are able to name a readily-available household product which teens are using to get high. The list is long and varied, but familiar.

Even if there were reason to be optimistic about the potential to dramatically reduce the flow of drugs into the United States through an interdiction strategy, going after supply cannot in itself be enough unless we are prepared to interdict the supply of readily-available commercial products that kids inhale to get high. Supply initiatives are essential, but they are no substitute for parental responsibility and fostering a new culture of intolerance toward illegal drug use.

Marijuana Is Teenagers' Drug of Choice

by Christopher S. Wren

About the author: *Christopher S. Wren is a staff writer for the* New York Times *daily newspaper.*

Nicole, a high school junior with short brown hair, soft eyes and a delicate chin, has smoked marijuana since she was 13 years old. Many of her friends at her Massachusetts high school use it too, and sometimes her father joins her.

"I smoke weed with my dad," Nicole, who is now 16, said. "Obviously he feels fine about it. Since I started smoking weed, we've gotten closer."

Marijuana has become so routine that Nicole admitted, "I smoke every single day."

Marijuana Use: More than Doubled

The rising use of illegal drugs by teen-agers like Nicole was confirmed in August 1996 by the Department of Health and Human Services, which reported that marijuana use by young people had more than doubled since 1992.

That report set off a running debate between President Bill Clinton and Bob Dole, his Republican challenger [for president in 1996], over the reasons for the increase. Mr. Dole accused Mr. Clinton of causing the increase by being inattentive to the drug problem. The President said the Republican-controlled Congress cut financing for his programs to reduce drug use.

Interviews with 30 teen-agers in New York and Massachusetts found that, indeed, marijuana use among the young appears to be increasing, perhaps at an even higher rate than the Government report and others suggest. In September 1996, the National Center on Addiction and Substance Abuse at Columbia University reported that by the time young people turn 17, 62 percent know someone who uses marijuana. Fewer than one in three said their schools were free of drugs.

The interviews also show that the political debate was not lost on teenagers.

Look at Bill Clinton, Nicole said. He smoked marijuana and became President. "He said that if he tried it again, he'd inhale," she said, referring to a quip in an interview Mr. Clinton gave in June 1992 to MTV, which Mr. Dole resurrected for his campaign.

Easy to Buy

During the interviews, conducted in October 1996, teen-agers from inner-city, working-class and suburban neighborhoods said marijuana can be as easy to buy as beer or cigarettes, often from schoolmates. The usual price is $5 a joint. "It takes one phone call," said Matt, a 16-year-old in Gloucester, Mass. A 16-year-old boy in Bronxville, N.Y., said he could find marijuana by walking a mile in any direction from his high school. Angel, 17, said it is sold under the counter in groceries and flower shops around his South Bronx neighborhood in New York City.

Most of the young people spoke on condition that they not be identified beyond first names and ages. Because drug use is illegal and because of fears about parental anger, a few asked for complete anonymity.

The Drug of Choice for Fun and Escape

Their comments confirmed that marijuana remained the overwhelming drug of choice, with cocaine and heroin use far less common.

Those who smoke marijuana said they started not because of peer pressure, but because it seemed fun and offered them temporary escape from the angst of growing up. They disparaged anti-drug advertisements and drug-prevention classes as ineffective and expressed skepticism that parents, teachers or other adults could make much difference.

Some teen-agers argued that marijuana could not be that bad if so many adults used it, and mentioned Mr. Clinton. "He must have tried it more than once," said Isa, a 17-year-old high school senior. "I bet maybe 50 percent of the Congress has tried it. I mean, some adults still use it. If you're smoking marijuana, you're not using drugs. I don't think that marijuana is the same thing as using cocaine or heroin."

The growing acceptance of marijuana is not lost on even younger students. "Some people tell you how it feels so good and stuff," said Ryan, a blond 13-year-old who reported that marijuana had piqued interest in his eighth-grade class.

> *"By the time young people turn 17, 62 percent know someone who uses marijuana."*

The teen-agers who grew up with drugs in New York City were less sanguine. "In my neighborhood, all you see is just drugs," said Angel, who has childhood memories of crack cocaine buyers lining up around his block. He tried marijuana when he was 13, and soon graduated to "blunts," cigars hollowed out and stuffed with marijuana. One day, he recalled, he smoked 11 blunts.

"I was really messing up," Angel said. "I wasn't going to school. I was disrespecting everybody." After running afoul of the law, he was accepted by Phoenix Academy, a residential high school in Yorktown Heights, N.Y., run by the drug treatment and prevention agency Phoenix House.

Misty's Drug Abuse

While most teen-age drug users confine themselves to marijuana, some confess to wider experimentation. "My mother did drugs and I said I never would, but when I was 12, I started doing drugs," said Misty, a dark-eyed high school senior in Massachusetts. "At the time I had a boyfriend who was much older than I."

By the time Misty turned 14, she found herself in a drug treatment program. "I was straight, like for two years," she said. "I didn't smoke weed or nothing. Then I went out with another guy, and I started doing it again."

Now 17, Misty said she has chopped up pills "real small" and sniffed them to get high. "My nose started bleeding, but I didn't care," she said. She laughed about how her latest boyfriend slipped LSD, a hallucinogen, into a beer she was drinking. And she has snorted cocaine.

"If it's given to you, obviously you're going to do it," Misty said. "A couple of weeks ago, I was really depressed and I did a line. I just hate it so much, but I keep doing it when I'm feeling all down and out." She feels high for a couple of seconds and then feels terrible, she said.

> *"While most teen-age drug users confine themselves to marijuana, some confess to wider experimentation."*

While surveys indicate that the majority of teen-agers do not use drugs, some abstainers admitted to feeling awkward around friends who do. "Sometimes they might think you're too good for them, like you have a prissy attitude," said Jennifer, a blond 16-year-old in Gloucester.

"There are a lot of kids who don't like drugs and who think it is actually stupid," Jennifer continued. "But who are we to say, 'Get that needle out of your arm'? When it comes down to stopping them from doing drugs, they've got to stop their own addictive behavior."

Social Acceptance and Curiosity

Ben, a lanky 17-year-old from Cambridge, attributed the experimentation at a younger age to lack of self-confidence. "In the eighth grade smoking marijuana would be an easy ticket to being cooler," he said. "I know there would be a good social result if I'd started smoking."

But marijuana users who were interviewed said that they started out of curiosity. "One day I was playing basketball and someone said, 'Let's get high,' so we did, and I loved it," said Matt, a sophomore who wore a baseball cap, brim backward, over his blond hair.

"I don't need to impress anybody," Matt said. "If I want to get high, I just get high. People say weed makes you stupid. I smoke weed, and I'm smart."

Errika, a 16-year-old sophomore in Gloucester, said some of her friends considered marijuana safer than tobacco. "People say, 'Why smoke cigarettes and get cancer when you can smoke weed and just lose a few brain cells?'" she said. As for marijuana's effect on academic performance, she said, "People will come to school high and say, 'Oh, I did awesome on my test.'"

But grades do suffer, said Raquel, a 16-year-old sophomore who flaunts an enamel marijuana pendant. "I started to be a straight-A student and then I started smoking pot and my grades went straight down," she said. "I'll go home now and not be able to do my homework."

Kay, a 15-year-old classmate who wore a studded leather collar and nose ring, said, "If you want to find out what it's like, you're going to do it."

Kay sloughed off criticism. "I've adjusted to friends who call us the freaks of the school," she said. "Someone told me we were worthless forms of life, and we just laughed in his face."

"Don't Use It"

Robert, a 20-year-old New Yorker who smoked his first joint at 13, attributed much of the teen-age drug use to rebellion. "When someone tells you not to do it, that makes you want to do it even more," he said. Marijuana was so abundant in his Queens neighborhood, Robert said, that "it's like going to the store and buying some gum or candy."

After being caught selling cocaine to support his appetite for blunts, he quit drugs and, like Angel, enrolled in Phoenix Academy. "Marijuana has really messed my mind up, because it makes it hard for me to remember something," said Robert, who is trying to finish high school. "If you want to become something in life, don't use it. If you don't want to become anything, go right ahead."

The advertising campaigns against illegal drugs pitch the same message, but few of the teen-agers seemed to take them seriously. Isa dismissed them as "a good laugh." And Mr. Clinton's warnings against drug use drew snickers. "For him to say don't do drugs, then to say he did it but he didn't inhale, that's a kind of far-fetched story," Jennifer said.

While professing indifference, many of the teen-agers acknowledged, however tacitly, that parents do matter. "If I had an addiction problem," Errika said, "I would trust my friends not to get my parents involved, because it would hurt them more than anything,"

In rejecting drugs, 15-year-old Daren credited his mother, a single parent struggling to bootstrap them both out of a tough Boston neighborhood. "I've been asked to try drugs and I say no, I don't want to start that," he said.

"If I was ever using drugs and my mom found out, it would be all over for me, because she's strict," Daren said with a hint of pride. "When my mom talks to me about drugs, she really puts a lot of emotion into it. She was choking up when she told me not to use drugs. I think it would really hurt my family."

Methamphetamine Use Is Spreading

by Daniel Sneider

About the author: *Daniel Sneider is a staff writer for the* Christian Science Monitor *newspaper in Boston.*

Set in a narrow valley in California's North Coast region, Potter Valley seems like an ideal place to raise a family. Cows and horses graze near pear orchards and grape vineyards. Children ride freely on their bikes.

Beneath this bucolic idyll, however, lies quite a different reality. Potter Valley, a small town of 3,000 people, is caught in the grip of a new drug epidemic that is as deadly and dangerous as any seen before. The drug is methamphetamine, a powerful stimulant that law-enforcement officials have labeled the "crack cocaine of the '90s."

Spreading Eastward

In regions like northern California, methamphetamine ranks second only to alcohol in usage. The drug is now spreading from the West, where it was concentrated, to places such as Iowa and Missouri. The abusers of this drug are typically blue-collar workers—truck drivers, waitresses, carpet layers—and are overwhelmingly white. Methamphetamine presents a deadly combination: It is cheap, easy to make, and creates a ferocious addiction that often triggers violence. From bitter experience, California officials have found close links between addiction and child abuse, including sexual abuse. At high levels of addiction, meth users become paranoid and liable to strike out in bizarre acts of brutality, even against family members.

"Crack cocaine simply bowled us over in the 1980s," retired Gen. Barry McCaffrey, the White House drug czar, told the *Monitor*. "We don't want that to happen again. Methamphetamine—the poor man's cocaine—may be an even worse insult to our family structure and our community life."

Federal and state authorities have launched a new effort to combat the growing epidemic. They are moving to try to cut off the supply of chemicals used to make the drug while putting pressure on the drug cartels producing and distributing it. At the same time, federal research money is being directed toward studying the drug and supporting innovative treatment programs. But these initial steps occur against a backdrop of neglect of the problem at a national level. People involved in both law enforcement and in treatment complain of meager resources to battle the plague. To date, few scientific studies have explored how the drug works and no specific therapy exists for its addicts. The public remains largely ignorant of its existence and of its effects.

A Wake-Up Call

It took the tragic death in 1996 of Raina Bo Shirley, a vivacious teen, to awaken the residents of Potter Valley to this evil in their midst. The region is a center of marijuana cultivation, and like many of the teens here, Raina was a casual pot smoker. But she was also, by the account of a close friend, a risk-taker who "wanted to have fun."

That desire led Raina to methamphetamine, a drug that had a significant adult following and was easily available in the town. According to court testimony, on a March afternoon, Raina and a friend went to a popular party spot along the Eel River with Arnoldo Jorge Manzo, who the Mendocino County sheriff's department identified in court as a drug dealer, and his cousin. The court record states that the girls were given methamphetamine, sexually assaulted, and left in a disoriented state. Raina

"Meth users become paranoid and liable to strike out in bizarre acts of brutality, even against family members."

disappeared and was discovered two weeks later, drowned in the river. There is a warrant for Mr. Manzo's arrest, and he is currently being sought by state and federal officials.

During those traumatic weeks of search parties and community meetings, Potter Valley folk learned how widely meth use had spread in their community. Mendocino County narcotics officers told them that the tree-covered hills around them harbored clandestine laboratories where the white powder was being "cooked" in large quantities by drug gangs for distribution throughout the state.

"This is a quiet town where everybody knows everybody—it was always a great place to live," says Connie Shepard, who grew up here and returned to raise a family. "I had no idea that our kids were putting that kind of junk in their system."

Carol Hill, on the other hand, was not surprised. "Families who didn't have kids in school were shocked," she says. But Ms. Hill had already "lost" her husband to meth (and jail) and is struggling to keep a teenage boy off drugs, using everything from heart-to-heart talks to random drug testing.

In the aftermath of Raina's tragedy, these women became leaders of programs organized under the Police Athletic League to keep teens busy with anything from theater to karate. Raina's grandfather, Ed Nickerman, is raising money to buy a house for a teen center. In a community that offers little entertainment, they hope this will reduce the lure of weekend parties "over the hill."

"This won't solve all of the problem, but it will solve a lot of the problem," says Mr. Nickerman, who also serves on the county school board.

But both organizers and the kids agree that while the programs are welcome, there is little evidence yet that they've made a dent in the problem. "The kids who are involved in things like that are not the kids using drugs," says high-schooler Amy Austin.

Residents have posted signs declaring "No Drugs in Potter," and have erected an elaborate billboard by the road entering the valley declaring "Distribution and Use of Drugs Prohibited."

County narcotics-control officers believe the glare of publicity has forced the labs out of the valley—for now. But the problem has not disappeared. Although high school kids say only a few of their peers use meth, they also acknowledge it is easy to find.

"We know the people who do it," says basketball team member Tisha Phillips. "People who don't want to bother with it stay away from them." And there is active hostility to the antidrug effort. In January 1997, someone removed many of the signs and sawed down the billboard, which was subsequently reinstalled. "Some people feel it's a joke," Ms. Hill says.

The problems of communities like Potter Valley are new but meth abuse is not. "We're in the third postwar methamphetamine epidemic in this country," says Michael Gorman, a scientist with the Alcohol and Drug Abuse Institute at the University of Washington and a leading expert on the drug.

Everyman's Drug

Amphetamines were developed early in this century and available by prescription in the 1930s for treatment of depression and other diseases. During World War II, soldiers on all sides used the drug. In the 1950s, amphetamine tablets were popularly known as "pep pills," used by athletes, truck drivers, and housewives.

A federal crackdown in the early 1960s on prescription abuses prompted the illicit production of methamphetamine, particularly in a liquid, injectable form. By the late 1960s, a second wave of abuse began in the Haight-Ashbury district of San Francisco, where it was known as "speed."

"I had no idea that our kids were putting that kind of junk in their system."

This outbreak was also controlled, but meth remained entrenched in the subculture of outlaw motorcycle gangs. The bikers used available chemicals, which they cooked in crude rural labs where the pungent odor associated with production could be concealed.

The third wave began in California in the 1980s, when meth spread in rural areas as a cheap alternative to cocaine. Federal authorities tried to control the chemicals used to manufacture methamphetamines. But traffickers switched to a different method based on chemicals used in products such as decongestants and diet pills, easily converted into an even more potent form known as D-methamphetamine.

> *"Meth labs are easily set up in motel rooms, trailers, or the backs of pickup trucks."*

Federal attempts to control the bulk trade in precursor chemicals in the late 1980s had an unfortunate consequence: They prompted the growing involvement of Mexican gangs who were distributors for the Colombian cocaine cartels. The gangs legally imported the chemicals from countries such as China and Switzerland, then smuggled them over the border into the US, creating a highly lucrative business. According to the Drug Enforcement Agency [DEA], an investment of $500 in chemicals yields about one pound of meth, selling for $12,000 in California and as much as $18,500 elsewhere in the US.

"The Mexicans brought a level of sophistication to the manufacture and distribution of this drug that the bikers did not have," says Randy Weaver, a researcher at the Department of Justice's National Drug Intelligence Center.

Rural Meth Shops

Meth labs are easily set up in motel rooms, trailers, or the backs of pickup trucks. The traffickers "cook" the chemicals for a few days, then move on, leaving behind toxic waste that can poison the soil and cost tens of thousands of dollars to clean up. The chemicals frequently explode, occasionally killing the "cooks" and innocent people. The majority of labs remain small operations, using "recipes" obtainable over the Internet and elsewhere to cook over-the-counter cold capsules and the like to derive ounces of meth. But federal and California narcotics officers report seeing larger labs in the last few years, which they say are usually run by Mexican nationals.

"We used to find ounces, now we are finding pounds," says an undercover narcotics officer in Mendocino County. "They're producing more and they're selling it cheaper," he says.

Meth use has moved beyond the traditional subcultures of users, such as bikers, gay men, and blue-collar, white males to college students, professionals, minorities, and especially women. It has also been encouraged by the use of less-potent legal stimulants associated with all-night "rave" dance parties popular in recent years.

More Hospital Admissions

The spread of meth use is reflected in a variety of statistics, including a massive increase in lab seizures. Perhaps the most horrifying evidence comes from hospitals in California, Arizona, and other states. More than 1,800 deaths were caused by meth abuse from 1992 to 1994. California emergency rooms saw a 49 percent increase in meth-related admissions in 1994 over 1995. Nationwide, admissions rose from less than 6,000 in 1991 to about 18,000 in 1994, according to the DEA.

A few years ago, Dr. Gorman was treating drug addicts in San Francisco when he noticed his case load shifting to meth. "I started scratching my head," he recounts. "There was no literature about how to deal with these people clinically." He noticed a particularly disturbing link between meth use, often by injection, and the spread of HIV infection.

John Brown, the police chief of Willits, Calif., has seen meth in town for 10 years or so. But in recent years, he says, people are using more of it, in more potent forms, and mixing it with other drugs, particularly alcohol. "In 90 percent of the cases of child abuse in our community, meth or alcohol, often together, are involved," says Chief Brown. The statistic is echoed in many California locales where this drug is prevalent.

Brown and other police began to encounter extreme acts of violence among high-intensity users known as "tweakers." In that state they are highly agitated and paranoid, ready to "go off any time, and when they do, they're extremely violent and extremely strong," he says.

In Willits in 1993, Trevor Harden, a meth addict who had been up all night using the drug, murdered four members of his family and then took his own life.

Drug Enforcement

Such incidents have served to galvanize a response. California Sen. Dianne Feinstein (D), at the prompting of both state and federal law-enforcement agencies, sponsored recently passed legislation to tighten controls over precursor chemicals and increase the criminal sentences for possession and distribution of the chemicals and the equipment used to make methamphetamines.

In January 1997, the White House Office of National Drug Control Policy sponsored a Western regional conference of law-enforcement officials, scientists, and treatment specialists to try to develop new strategies for dealing with meth. "This is the single biggest drug challenge we have today in California," Attorney General Daniel Lungren told the meeting, appealing for more federal resources.

> *"This is the single biggest drug challenge we have today in California."*

Law-enforcement officials are focusing on the four Mexican cartels known to be involved in trafficking. "Mexico has to take some steps to control its own border," Senator Feinstein says.

But even federal drug enforcement officials acknowledge that methamphetamine is largely a home-grown problem. Indeed, the DEA has identified California as a "source country" for the drug.

"The biggest shortcoming is drug prevention strategies focused on methamphetamines," General McCaffrey says. "If you don't have a strategy to educate the threatened subpopulations about what's going to happen to you, then why would you think adding 35 more DEA agents is going to solve the problem?"

Resources to Combat Meth Addiction

Equally lacking is scientific research and funding for treatment of addicts. "We need medical forms of intervention, and we need some therapeutic forms of intervention specifically targeted on methamphetamines," McCaffrey says.

The problem is particularly acute in rural counties, where meth use is concentrated and resources are scarce. In the Mendocino County seat of Ukiah, for example, at least 100 people are on the waiting list for admission to the main drug-treatment program, most of them women. "We have waiting lists of people who want treatment but we have a prison bed for each of them," says Ned Walsh, administrator of the county alcohol and drug treatment program.

The recent attention to the problem has cheered researchers like Gorman, who has traveled to Washington many times trying to raise awareness. But he and others on the front lines of this battle worry that the focus of resources on cocaine and other drugs has created a bureaucratic resistance to recognizing the severity of the meth epidemic.

"There are state and federal resources available if people will get it together to move those resources," Gorman says. "What is it going to take?"

There Is No Youth Marijuana Crisis

by Paul Armentano

About the author: *Paul Armentano is the publications director for the Washington, D.C.–based National Organization for the Reform of Marijuana Laws (NORML), which advocates the legalization of marijuana.*

According to federal politicians, drug prohibitionists, and the majority of the national news media, adolescent marijuana use is soaring toward "epidemic" proportions. This claim has been made so frequently that many people are unaware that there exists any serious debate on the issue. But there is little tangible evidence behind the headlines. This latest round of reefer madness appears to be nothing more than a ploy to encourage legislators to stiffen penalties against adult users.

No Doubling of Users

Claim 1: Marijuana use among teens has doubled since 1992.

This statement is both misleading and inaccurate. The standard yardstick of adolescent marijuana use has for more than 20 years been the Monitoring the Future study conducted at the University of Michigan's Institute for Social Research. Each year, this study tracks lifetime marijuana use among high school seniors. In 1995, the report showed, nearly 42% of all high school seniors had used marijuana at least once. This figure is an increase from the 32.6% who reported having tried marijuana in 1992—the lowest rate in the study's history—but it is hardly a doubling. In fact, current use rates are less than 2% higher than they were as recently as 1990, when the figure stood at 40.7%.

Some prohibitionists attempt to confuse this issue by pointing to other, more specific data (e.g., daily use among eighth graders, monthly use among tenth graders, etc.) that may illustrate a sharper increase in marijuana use for that category alone. However, as the Monitoring the Future statistics illustrate, *lifetime* use of marijuana among high school seniors has remained predominantly the same for years, even as other age groups' patterns of use have varied. In all, the

From Paul Armentano, "The New Reefer Madness," *Liberty*, January 1997. Reprinted by permission.

percentage of graduating high school seniors who have tried marijuana has remained between one-third and one-half for nearly three decades.

Hardly an Epidemic

Claim 2: Today, our children are smoking more dope than at any time in recent memory.

Apparently, the prohibitionists don't possess very long memories. Data from both the Monitoring the Future study and the National Household Survey indicate that current rates of adolescent marijuana use, both regular and lifetime, are well below the levels of a few years ago. According to the Monitoring the Future study, lifetime prevalence of marijuana use among high school seniors peaked in 1979 at 60%, a figure almost 50% higher than today's rates. During this same

> "Lifetime *use of marijuana among high school seniors has remained predominantly the same for years.*"

year, according to the National Household Survey on Drug Abuse, the percentage of youths aged 12–17 who reported regularly using marijuana (defined as once within the past month) also peaked, measuring 16.7%. Put in historical perspective, the 1979 figure is more than twice as high as today's "epidemic" of 8.2%. Moreover, today's rate is only marginally higher than the percentage of adolescents who regularly consumed marijuana in 1988 (6.4%), at the height of the drug war and the "Just Say No" campaign. Lastly, it must be noted that changes in the methodology of the Household Survey in 1994 make accurate comparisons difficult.

A Misleading Assertion

Claim 3: Users are starting younger than ever before.

Reports from the Monitoring the Future study have indicated that marijuana use among eighth and tenth graders has risen since 1992. This is not particularly surprising, as the study began surveying eighth and tenth graders only one year earlier. Not coincidentally, 1991 and 1992 were the lowest years ever recorded for adolescent marijuana use. Since then, use of marijuana has risen for adolescents of all ages. The truth is, we really don't know whether today's teens are using marijuana at a younger age than ever before, because Monitoring the Future has no data from the 1970s or 1980s to compare it to. Moreover, weighing today's figures against percentages of eighth and tenth graders taken in 1992—the year reported adolescent marijuana use rates stood at their lowest in history—serves little scientific purpose and is highly misleading.

The National Household Survey has attempted to use data from 1991–1993 to extrapolate the average age at which adolescents began using marijuana. The Survey notes that these estimates should be "interpreted with caution" and may not portray an accurate answer to this question. Nevertheless, the Survey's estimates indicate that today's figures regarding age-specific rates of first marijuana use are not unique, but rather imitate patterns exhibited in the mid-1970s and early 1980s.

Not a Gateway Drug

Claim 4: Today's youthful marijuana users are tomorrow's cocaine addicts.

According to literature from the National Institute on Drug Abuse (NIDA), the majority of marijuana users do not become dependent on cannabis or move on to other illegal drugs. This stands to reason when one realizes that an estimated 71 million Americans have experimented with marijuana at some point in their lives, and that the majority of them never went on to use cocaine. Therefore, while it may be true that some cocaine users did first use marijuana as adolescents, the far more important fact is that the overwhelming number of teen marijuana users never go on to use cocaine or any other illegal narcotic.

In addition, federal literature suggests that the minority of marijuana users who do graduate to harder drugs such as cocaine do so not because of marijuana use, but because of marijuana prohibition. "Using marijuana puts children and teens in contact with people who are users and sellers of other drugs," states *Marijuana: What Parents Need to Know,* a 1995 pamphlet distributed by the U.S. Department of Health and Human Services. "So there is more of a chance for a marijuana user to be exposed and urged to try more drugs."

Support for this theory comes from the Netherlands, where marijuana can be purchased openly in government-regulated "coffee shops" designed specifically to keep young marijuana users from the illegal markets where harder drugs are sold. In contrast to the U.S., where 16% of youthful marijuana users admit to having tried cocaine, only 1.8% of young Dutch marijuana users have tried cocaine. It

> *"The majority of marijuana users do not become dependent on cannabis or move on to other illegal drugs."*

appears that when the cannabis markets are effectively separated from those for harder illegal drugs, marijuana is not a gateway drug, but a "terminus" one.

No Higher Potency

Claim 5: The marijuana adolescents are smoking today is much more potent than the marijuana their parents consumed.

Not so, according to the data provided by the Potency Monitoring Project at the University of Mississippi, the government-funded program that has been analyzing samples of marijuana for THC content since the mid-1970s. (There are no known measures of THC content prior to 1968, and only a few plants were assayed before 1972. THC is the main psychoactive ingredient in marijuana.) This data, based on analysis of over 23,200 samples, indicates that current average marijuana potency remains under 3% THC, essentially within the same range as the samples assayed by the government during the middle and late 1970s. In addition, there are many examples of marijuana samples from the same period, measured independently by companies such as PharmChem Laboratories, that frequently range from 2–5% THC, with some as high as 14%.

"We try to tell [those who claim that marijuana potency has greatly increased] that there's no study to support the belief that potency is greatly different," a spokesman from NIDA, speaking on a condition of anonymity, told the *Arkansas Democrat-Gazette* in 1995. "I thought [marijuana opponents] had stopped saying that."

Relatively Harmless

Claim 6: Adolescent marijuana use poses great harm to society.

America survived the 1970s and will survive the 1990s. While it would be silly to suggest that marijuana is totally harmless, or to advocate that adolescents *should* consume it, the fact remains that moderate marijuana use is relatively harmless and poses far less cost to society than do either cigarettes or alcohol. Today—as in 1977, when President Jimmy Carter recommended federal decriminalization—marijuana prohibition causes far more harm than marijuana itself does.

We may never know why adolescent marijuana use rates fluctuate over time or to what extent social stigmas and social norms regarding cannabis influence the accuracy of self-reporting, the sole source of these data. We do know that adolescence is a period filled with experimentation and that recreational marijuana use, for good or bad, is sometimes a part of this experience. Young people, as well as all Americans, should be informed of the scientific evidence about marijuana so that they can make knowledgeable decisions about both their own drug use and the future of American drug policy.

The claims of rapidly rising and near-epidemic rates of adolescent marijuana use simply do not stand up to close examination. When put in historical perspective, today's figures warrant only mild concern. They certainly do not justify intensifying the war against adult marijuana consumers, a battle that resulted in more than 482,000 arrests in 1994 alone. We do not arrest

> *"The fact remains that moderate marijuana use is relatively harmless and poses far less cost to society than do either cigarettes or alcohol."*

responsible adult alcohol drinkers because we want adolescents to avoid alcohol; neither should we arrest responsible adult marijuana smokers to protect children from smoking marijuana.

Marijuana Use Does Not Lead to Harder Drugs

by Lynn Zimmer and John P. Morgan

About the authors: *Lynn Zimmer is a sociology professor at Queens College in New York City. John P. Morgan is a professor at the City University of New York Medical School.*

Marijuana does not cause people to use hard drugs. What the gateway theory presents as a causal explanation is a statistical association between common and uncommon drugs, an association that changes over time as different drugs increase and decrease in prevalence. Marijuana is the most popular illegal drug in the United States today. Therefore, people who have used less popular drugs, such as heroin, cocaine, and LSD, are likely to have also used marijuana. Most marijuana users never use any other illegal drug. Indeed, for the large majority of people, marijuana is a *terminus* rather than a *gateway* drug.

Supposed Gateways

Proponents of the gateway theory, formerly known as the "stepping-stone hypothesis," argue that even if marijuana itself is not very dangerous, marijuana leads people to use other, more dangerous drugs. In the 1950s, marijuana was said to be a gateway to heroin, and in the 1960s, a gateway to LSD. Today, marijuana is discussed primarily as a gateway to cocaine.

People who use cocaine, a relatively unpopular drug, are likely to have used the more popular drug, marijuana. Marijuana users are also more likely than non-users to have had previous experience with legal drugs, such as alcohol, tobacco, and caffeine. Alcohol, tobacco, and caffeine do not cause people to use marijuana. Marijuana does not cause people to use heroin, LSD, or cocaine.

The relationship between marijuana and other drugs varies across societies. Within the United States, the relationship varies across age groups and substances, and from one social group to another. Over time, as any particular drug increases or decreases in popularity, its relationship to marijuana changes. While marijuana use was increasing in the 1960s and 1970s, heroin use was de-

Excerpted from Chapter 4 of *Marijuana Myths, Marijuana Facts* by Lynn Zimmer and John P. Morgan (New York: Lindesmith Center), © Lynn Zimmer and John P. Morgan. Reprinted by permission. The complete version of the book *Marijuana Myths, Marijuana Facts* includes footnotes that support the authors' assertions.

clining. During the past twenty years, as marijuana use rates fluctuated, rates for LSD remained about the same. Cocaine became popular in the early 1980s as marijuana use was declining; later in the decade, both marijuana and cocaine use declined. During the past few years, marijuana use has increased while the decline in cocaine use has continued.

Only One in One Hundred

Figure 1 illustrates the changing relationship between marijuana use and cocaine use over time. At the height of cocaine's popularity in 1986, 33 percent of high school seniors who had used marijuana had also tried cocaine. By 1995, only 14 percent of marijuana users had tried cocaine. Even when marijuana users try cocaine, they do not necessarily become regular users. In fact, very few do. As shown in figure 2, of the seventy-two million Americans who have used marijuana, about twenty million have tried cocaine. Of this twenty million, about 30 percent used cocaine only once or twice. Only 17 percent used cocaine more than one hundred times. In other words, for every one hundred people who have used marijuana, *only one* is a current regular user of cocaine.

Figure 1. Percentage of Marijuana Users Ever Trying Cocaine (High School Seniors, 1975–1995).

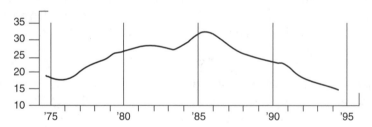

Source: *National Survey Results on Drug Use from the Monitoring the Future Study, 1975–1995*, National Institute on Drug Abuse.

The probability of trying cocaine is not distributed equally across the population of marijuana users. Teens who use marijuana occasionally, and use no illicit drugs other than marijuana, are unlikely to ever try cocaine. Indeed, most teens who try marijuana never even become regular users of marijuana. In 1994, among twelve- to seventeen-year-olds who had tried marijuana, 60 percent had used it fewer than twelve times and about 40 percent had tried it only once or twice.

> *"Even when marijuana users try cocaine, they do not necessarily become regular users."*

Studies show that most teens who try cocaine have had many previous drug experiences. Most began using alcohol and marijuana at an earlier age than

---

Figure 2. Very Few Marijuana Users Become Regular Users of Cocaine.

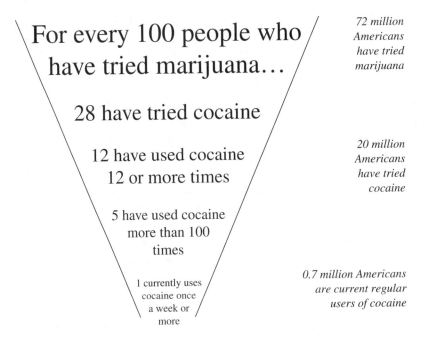

72 million Americans have tried marijuana

For every 100 people who have tried marijuana…

28 have tried cocaine

20 million Americans have tried cocaine

12 have used cocaine 12 or more times

5 have used cocaine more than 100 times

1 currently uses cocaine once a week or more

0.7 million Americans are current regular users of cocaine

Data from *National Household Survey on Drug Abuse: Population Estimates 1994*, Rockville, MD: U.S. Department of Health and Human Services (1995); *National Household Survey on Drug Abuse: Main Findings 1994*, Rockville, MD: U.S. Department of Health and Human Services (1996).

---

their peers, and most continue to use both alcohol and marijuana frequently. Most also tried numerous other illicit drugs before trying cocaine. One study, looking at adults who had been marijuana users in high school, found that over 80 percent of those who eventually tried cocaine were already multiple-drug users. They regularly used alcohol, tobacco, and marijuana, and had also tried stimulants, sedatives, and psychedelics.

Few adolescents become early multiple-drug users, and those who do differ from their peers in a number of ways. They are more likely to be poor, more likely to live in neighborhoods where illicit drug use is prevalent, less likely to come from stable homes, less likely to be successful at school, and more likely to have psychological problems. Most multiple-drug users engage in a variety of deviant and delinquent activities prior to using legal or illegal drugs. In other words, within the general population of adolescent marijuana users, there is a deviant minority who become multiple-drug users.

Different Effects

In the 1970s, Gabriel Nahas claimed that marijuana caused users to seek stimulation from "more potent drugs" by disrupting "the delicate chemical equilibrium in the brain." This theory has no empirical basis. The effects of heroin and co-caine are not bigger than those of marijuana; they are qualitatively different. Un-like heroin and cocaine, which produce an effect by increasing dopamine in the brain's "pleasure-reward substrate," there is strong evidence that marijuana has little or no effect on dopamine's availability in this system. In short, marijuana does not prime the brain for new psychopharmacological experiences.

> *"Marijuana does not prime the brain for new psychopharmacological experiences."*

A report by the Center on Addiction and Substance Abuse (CASA) says that youthful marijuana users are eighty-five times more likely than non-users to use cocaine. CASA's calculation is based on marijuana and cocaine prevalence data from 1991. To obtain the eighty-five times "risk factor," CASA divided the proportion of marijuana users who had *ever tried cocaine* (17 percent) by the proportion of cocaine users who had *never used marijuana* (0.2 percent). The "risk factor" is large not because so many marijuana users experiment with cocaine, but because very few people try cocaine without trying marijuana first.

No Theory

In the end, the gateway theory is not a theory at all. It is simply a description of the typical sequence in which multiple-drug users initiate the use of high-prevalence and low-prevalence drugs. A similar statistical relationship exists between other kinds of common and uncommon related activities. For example, most people who ride a motorcycle (a fairly rare activity) have ridden a bicycle (a fairly common activity). Indeed, the prevalence of motorcycle riding among people who have never ridden a bicycle is probably extremely low. However, bicycle riding does not cause motorcycle riding, and increases in the former will not lead automatically to increases in the latter. Nor will increases in mari-juana use lead automatically to increases in the use of cocaine or other drugs.

The Heroin Abuse Problem Is Exaggerated

by Jack Shafer

About the author: *Jack Shafer is the deputy editor of* Slate, *an on-line magazine published by Microsoft Corporation.*

In July 1996, the press reprised one of its favorite stories: Heroin is back. The news hook was the death [in New York City] of Smashing Pumpkins side man Jonathan Melvoin, 34, while shooting scag in a Park Avenue hotel. The *Washington Post* Page One obit on Melvoin claimed—without substantiation—"a resurgence in heroin use in the '90s," while the *New York Times* asserted that the "heroin vogue has been building since at least 1993 and shows no signs of ebbing." *Trainspotting*, the 1996 movie about young Scottish junkies, provided another useful occasion for noting this alleged trend.

Always Coming Back

"Smack Is Back"? For the press, smack is *always* back. It never goes away, but it's always returning. Boarding the Nexis [article database service] wayback machine, we find that nearly every publication in America has sounded the heroin clarion yearly since 1989: the *New York Times* ("Latest Drug of Choice for Abusers Brings New Generation to Heroin," 1989); *U.S. News & World Report* ("The Return of a Deadly Drug Called Horse," 1989); the *San Francisco Chronicle* ("Heroin Making a Resurgence in the Bay Area," 1990); the *New York Times* ("Heroin Is Making Comeback," 1990); *Time* magazine ("Heroin Comes Back," 1990); the *Los Angeles Times* ("As Cocaine Comes off a High, Heroin May Be Filling Void," 1991); the *Cleveland Plain Dealer* ("Police, Social Workers Fear Heroin 'Epidemic,'" 1992); *Rolling Stone* ("Heroin: Back on the Charts," 1992); the *Seattle Times* ("Heroin People: Deadly Drug Back in Demand," 1992); NPR [National Public Radio] ("Heroin Makes Comeback in United States," 1992); *Newsweek* ("Heroin Makes an Ominous Comeback," 1993); the Trenton *Record* ("A Heroin Comeback," 1993); the *Washington Post* ("Smack Dabbling," 1994); the *New York Times* ("Heroin Finds a New Market

Along Cutting Edge of Style," 1994); *USA Today* ("Smack's Back," 1994); the *Buffalo News* ("More Dopes Picking Heroin," 1994); the Fort Lauderdale *Sun-Sentinel* ("Heroin Makes a Comeback," 1995); the [New Orleans] *Times-Picayune* ("Heroin Is Back as Major Problem," 1996); the *Arkansas Democrat-Gazette* ("State Gets Deadly Dose as Heroin Reappears," 1996); *Rolling Stone* again ("Heroin," 1996); and the *Los Angeles Times* ("Heroin's New Popularity Claims Unlikely Victims," 1996).

The granddaddy of the genre appeared in *Newsweek* ("Middle-Class Junkies," Aug. 10, 1981), with language that reads as fresh today as it did then. We learn that heroin has breached its ghetto quarantine: "[C]hildren of affluence are venturing where once the poor and desperate nodded out. The drug is being retailed at rock clubs, at Hollywood parties, and among lunch-time crowds in predominately white business districts." As always, part of the problem is a glut of white powder: "[S]heer abundance is prompting concern about a potential 'epidemic' spilling across demographic divides." And heroin purity is increasing dramatically: "Purity levels as high as 90 percent have been found in seized wholesale caches, with street-level purities averaging up to 20 percent—around six times the typical strength of the 1970 Turkish blend."

Estimating Heroin's Purity

Having hit 90 percent in 1981, you wouldn't think that heroin purity could keep rising. But for the press, it has. The *Washington Post*'s story about Melvoin reported that heroin purity has risen from "as low as 4 percent in past decades to upward of 70 percent today," while the *Los Angeles Times*' piece noted that heroin had gone "from 4 percent [purity] in 1980 to 40 percent in 1995." After Melvoin died, the Associated Press reported that the heroin he shot was 60 percent to 70 percent pure.

Depending on where you drop the Nexis plumb line, you can find references to more potent street heroin in the recent past. A 1989 *New York Times* story pegged the potency of heroin at 45 percent. In 1990, the *Washington Post* placed average purity at 30 percent to 40 percent, and in 1992, the *San Diego Union-Tribune* quoted a Drug Enforcement Administration official source who said that black tar heroin being seized was now topping the scales at 70 percent pure. A 1996 government study puts purity at 59 percent, so if the DEA was right a few years ago, recent purity actually has declined somewhat.

> *"For the press, smack is **always** back."*

What Causes Overdoses

There is good evidence that potency isn't the most significant risk factor in overdose deaths. A study of heroin overdoses in Washington, D.C., the findings of which were published by the *Journal of Forensic Sciences* (1989), found no relationship between heroin purity and either death by overdose or nonfatal overdose. (On the night that Melvoin shot that 60 to 70 percent heroin and died, Pumpkins drummer Jimmy Chamberlin shot the same junk and survived.) The researchers attributed most overdoses to intermittent or post-addiction use of heroin—meaning that people who OD'd tended to misjudge tolerance when returning to the drug. Another risk factor that never gets enough ink in the heroin-obsessed media is the danger of using heroin in combination with alcohol. The mixture has an additive effect: A drinker could spike himself with a lower-than-lethal dose and still OD.

What do we really know about heroin use? For one thing, the federal government's National Drug Control Strategy for 1996 says that the addict population is basically stable. It reports that the number of "casual users" (less than weekly) of heroin came down by more than half between 1988 and 1993 (539,000 to 229,000), the most recent year measured, while the number of "heavy users" (at least weekly) dipped from 601,000 to 500,000. One statistic feeding the heroin "revival" stories is the increasing number of emergency-room visits by people who mention heroin as a reason for seeking ER treatment. But the statistics, which come from the government's Drug Abuse Warning Network (DAWN) survey, come with a disclaimer suggesting that the explanation may be multiple visits by aging druggies who are using the ER for a variety of health problems.

> *"The number of 'casual users' (less than weekly) of heroin came down by more than half between 1988 and 1993."*

My bet is that when the medical examiner releases his report on Jonathan Melvoin, it will disclose that the smashed pumpkin was drinking booze while shooting, a fatal error that pre-'50s addicts almost never made. We'll learn that Melvoin—like the press—was an amateur who didn't really know what he was doing with heroin. [Editor's note: An autopsy revealed the presence of alcohol and heroin in Melvoin's body.]

A "Crack Baby" Crisis Does Not Exist

by Lillie Wilson

About the author: *Lillie Wilson is a writer for the* Greensburg Tribune-Review, *a daily newspaper distributed in western Pennsylvania.*

Like all vigorous clinicians, Rick Solomon had read the literature. By the late-1980s, he knew all about the reported surge of urban newborns exposed to cocaine in the womb—a species the media would soon dub "crack babies."

Solomon, director of Allegheny Behavioral and Child Development Services at Allegheny General Hospital (AGH), was in a special position to care. He's a developmental expert who treats hundreds of kids a year.

But he was hardly alone. Across the river, researcher Nancy Day of the Western Psychiatric Institute & Clinic started following case histories of such children, research necessary to answer questions being raised everywhere: What kind of harm would this harsh, new drug do to the kids prenatally exposed? Would they suffer permanent brain damage? Learning deficits? Emotional problems?

A Large Misconception

Some 10 years later, Solomon, Day and other scientists find themselves battling what has turned out to be perhaps the most sweeping misconception to plague the nation's crack epidemic: That of the doomed crack child. "It's an urban legend," says Solomon, who has been on duty at the AGH neonatal ward throughout his tenure.

That's not to say cocaine use during pregnancy isn't harmful. But the presumed connection between being born on crack and later learning and behavior problems has not materialized, Solomon says.

Most new research concurs. "We think it is clear now, from a multitude of studies, that the effect of prenatal cocaine exposure is minimal at birth and is probably limited to minor growth deficits," Day wrote in 1993 during ongoing research.

From Lillie Wilson, "Myths and Mystery About 'Crack Babies,'" Greensburg (Pa.) *Tribune-Review*, August 25, 1996. Reprinted with permission.

Today, Day's research subjects—about 300 children born at Magee-Women's Hospital—have reached 6 and 7 years of age. When you analyze the results correctly, she says, the differences between those children exposed versus not exposed *in utero* all but evaporate. "The phenomenon of the 'crack baby' just isn't there," Day says flatly.

Effects of Drugs at Birth and Afterward				
Affliction	*Heroin*	*Cocaine*	*Cigarettes*	*Alcohol*
Decreased birthweight	•	•	•	•
Stunted growth (newborn)		•	•	•
Mental retardation				•
Central nervous system problems (newborn)	•	•	•	•
Later education/behavior problems				•
Newborn withdrawal	•			
Physical deformities				•

Source: *Tribune-Review*, August 25, 1996.

But the protests by Day, Solomon and their conscientious medical colleagues may be falling on ears already deafened by the media blast—a chorus that preceded any reliable data and that lasted for years, filtering into education and social work journals as well as the popular press.

The television camera crews had already hit the neonatal intensive care wards long before Day and other researchers reached their conclusions.

An Oversensationalized Scare

Powered by the swell of popular outrage, school officials, politicians and policy wonks spun anecdotes and theories together and declaimed a general prognosis: "Crack babies," the projection went, would turn out to be neurologically wasted for life—a "biological underclass," one educator wrote—who would overwhelm the school system's special education rooms and strain the welfare system.

"Professionals who work with children are seeing alarming signals," U.S. Sen. Christopher J. Dodd, D-Connecticut, told a special subcommittee in 1990, basing his remarks on reported interviews with social workers and teachers. "For these children and society, the future costs of perinatal exposure are staggering. . . . At a minimum, cocaine-exposed children will cost this nation $100 billion in remedial medical and developmental costs over the next decade."

> *"The phenomenon of the 'crack baby' just isn't there."*

In 1987, Los Angeles' Unified School District set up a special, multimillion-dollar curriculum designed especially for identified crack kids. In 1989, the Florida Department of Human Resources estimated it would need $40,000 per child to get crack babies ready to start school because of the kids' impairments.

Such initiatives were based on a tiny dose of data and a large dose of hysteria, reflects Columbia University's Donald E. Hutchings, emeritus editor of leading toxicology journals. The crack baby scare, Hutchings now agrees, "was greatly oversensationalized on the basis of some very preliminary observations."

Psychologist Dan Griffith, who helped generate some of those observations while at the National Center for Perinatal Addiction in Chicago, is today racked with regret. It's not so much over his inadvertent role in helping to spin a false stereotype as over the wild reaction of the media—and over the stereotype's victims: Those children born into crack households who have been labeled losers, or worse.

Griffith, who holds workshops in prenatal drug exposure for foster parents and teachers, is used to a common refrain. He'll ask workshop participants to describe the child they know came from a cocaine-using mother.

"They'll say, 'Oh, he's alright. He's not like those other drug-exposed children,'" Griffith says. "That's how powerful the stereotype is."

School officials, on the whole, have already been sold. Many admit the expectation of crack-baby hordes swelling the special education rolls was purely speculative. But they contend their student bodies have indeed changed, and not for the better.

Behavior Problems

In the 1990s, teachers and administrators have noted marked increases in the number of children with behavior problems and in the extent and disruptiveness of those problems, says Henry Benz, director of pupil affairs for the Pittsburgh Public Schools. "Some of these children are aggressive, and they're aggressive beyond reason," says Benz. "If you have one or two of these kids in a class, it can turn the classroom into chaos. . . .

"What we do see is kids who are more bizarrely learning disabled, more bizarrely behavior disordered,

> *"The crack baby scare . . . 'was greatly oversensationalized on the basis of some very preliminary observations.'"*

than anything we've seen before," Benz says. "I don't know what it comes from."

It's not that the medical experts reject such reports. Clinicians like Solomon at AGH even reaffirm the reports, but most often point to a different cause: The family dissolution and poor caretaking that comes from any of poverty's social stresses, including transience and alcoholism as well as drug use.

"I see it every day. I see the effects of increasing poverty on kids," Solomon says of the children who come through his clinic. "What you have is a growing concentration of children living in poverty—about 22 to 23 percent by the last census. . . .

"In a way, it would be nice if you could point your finger at mothers hooked on crack cocaine and say that was the real problem. But it's not. That's just an easy answer," Solomon says. "The real problem is the increasing neglect of the poor, which is showing up in disrupted families."

Myths About Crack

A number of other popular fictions about crack abound. Some of the most prevalent:

• *Crack babies account for the surge in Attention Deficit Disorder in the schools.* Not only does no research bear this out, but the numbers don't square. The National Institute on Drug Abuse in Rockville, Md., estimates that in 1992, 1.1 percent of mothers used cocaine during pregnancy. Professional estimates of Attention Deficit Disorder in the schools veer between 5 and 10 percent.

• *Cocaine is the worst drug to take during pregnancy.* Whereas no serious long-standing mental and physical deficits have been traced to intrauterine cocaine exposure in well-controlled research, extreme deficits have been linked to alcohol exposure and mild deficits (mainly growth retardation) to nicotine exposure from cigarette smoking. "There's little doubt that as far as all the drugs' effects on the fetus go, the very worst drug is alcohol," Griffith says.

> *"No serious long-standing mental and physical deficits have been traced to intrauterine cocaine exposure in well-controlled research."*

• *Crack is more addictive than powder cocaine because it is "purer."* Crack is chemically the same drug as cocaine and delivers the same chemical stimulants to the brain. Crack is indeed more addictive, but only because the delivery system is faster.

Addiction specialists contend it's the speed of the high that gets people hooked so fast and so hard. Crack, when smoked, packs a quicker punch because it is absorbed through the lungs and shot directly to the brain through the left side of the heart. Unlike cocaine injected into a vein, crack does not have to circulate through the body first, explains addictions expert Mark Fuller of Blue Cross of Western Pennsylvania.

The speedy delivery makes a crack smoker high within 10 seconds, much faster than he'd get by shooting or snorting. It's the rapid rush, the quick peak and the short duration of the high that leaves the user with an irresistible craving for more once the drug wears off.

As for purity, although powder cocaine is notorious for being cut with noxious additives (including strychnine), crack—which is essentially cooked from liquid freebase cocaine—can also be laced with dangerous adulterants.

• *The crack epidemic is an African-American phenomenon.* Nationally, white crack smokers far outnumber their black counterparts, according to the 1994 National Household Survey on Drug Abuse performed by the U.S. Department of Health and Human Services. Whereas approximately 2.8 million whites had smoked crack by the end of the survey year, only about 782,000 blacks had done so.

The percent-per-population breakdown produces a higher per capita sampling rate for blacks than whites—3.3 percent versus 1.8 percent.

Chapter 2

Should Drug Testing Be Allowed?

Chapter Preface

Workplace drug testing has become an increasingly common practice. Today, 98 percent of America's largest companies use drug testing to screen potential employees, and many firms conduct random drug tests of their workers.

Proponents of employee drug testing argue that such tests reduce and deter substance abuse among workers, improve workplace safety and productivity, and reduce health-care costs attributed to drug abuse. According to Drug Watch International, "Drug testing is an effective and humane method to deter and to detect drug use. It has been overwhelmingly supported by the courts." Drug Watch International and other advocates credit drug testing for helping reduce workplace drug abuse by half between the mid-1980s and the mid-1990s.

But critics maintain that workplace drug testing violates employees' privacy, is often inaccurate, and does not reveal whether employees are actually impaired while working. The American Civil Liberties Union (ACLU) writes, "Random drug testing is pervasive, but is it fair? Are the tests accurate? Do they deter or prevent drug use? The ACLU's answer to all three questions is: no." Opponents of employee drug testing point out that the American Management Association and the National Academy of Sciences each have concluded that there is no survey data or scientific evidence to support the claim that drug testing deters drug use among employees.

While proponents and critics agree on the importance of a drug-free workplace, they disagree on which methods should be used to achieve such an environment. The authors in this chapter debate whether drug testing should be allowed.

Drug Testing Improves the Workplace

by Mark A. de Bernardo

About the author: *Mark A. de Bernardo, a labor and employment attorney, is the executive director of the Institute for a Drug-Free Workplace in Washington, D.C.*

How big is America's drug problem?

Enormous. The U.S. government reports that 9.7 million Americans used marijuana and 1.9 million used cocaine in the last month. Today, drugs often-times are *stronger* (marijuana harvested recently in northern California had 22 times the THC content of late '60s marijuana, THC being the psychoactive in-gredient in the drug), *cheaper* (a "hit" of crack is still available for as little as $5 in many cities), and *more lethal* (record numbers of overdoses and medical emergencies in recent years) than ever before. Perhaps most tragically, as many as 375,000 "coke babies" have been born in the United States in one year. Clearly, drug abuse is at crisis levels.

The Cost to Business

But is it business's problem?

Sixty-six percent of the Americans who engage in illicit drug use are em-ployed. Based on government figures, that means 6.5 million regular marijuana users and 1.25 million regular cocaine users are in the U.S. work force. Many of the "regular" drug users are—or will become—chronic drug abusers and ad-dicts who are even more likely to compromise the workplace in numerous ways: decreased productivity and increased accidents, medical claims, absen-teeism, product defects, insurance costs, and employee theft, to name a few. Roger Smith, the former chairman of General Motors, said drug abuse cost GM $1 billion a year. Obviously, the economic cost of drug abuse to business is enormous; the human cost is even greater.

What are employers doing about the drug problem?

First, employers are adopting *anti-drug abuse policies,* communicating them to employees and job applicants, and enforcing them. Those who violate the

Excerpted from Mark A. de Bernardo, *What Every Employee Should Know About Drug Abuse*, pamphlet of the Institute for a Drug-Free Workplace, 5th ed., 1995. Reprinted with permission.

policies are subject to adverse employment action up to and including dismissal.

Second, many employers have implemented *comprehensive drug education and drug awareness programs.* These include supervisor training and educational presentations and materials for employees and their families. It is critically important that Americans recognize the symptoms and dangers of drug abuse, and the legitimate stake employers and employees have in preventing it.

> *"The economic cost of drug abuse to business is enormous; the human cost is even greater."*

Third, many employers have implemented *drug testing programs* for one or more classes of job applicants or employees. Drug testing can be an effective component of a comprehensive drug abuse prevention program, one whose success in deterrence and detection of drug problems is vital.

Finally, company-provided *employee assistance and rehabilitation programs* can be the last and best hope many chronic drug abusers and addicts will *ever* have to go straight. Employee assistance programs (EAPs) can be humane, effective, *and* cost-effective. . . .

The Employer's Responsibility

But is it any of an employer's business what an employee does in the privacy of his or her own home on a Saturday night?

First of all, there is no Constitutional or other legally protected right to engage in *illegal* conduct in the privacy of one's own home or anyone else's.

Secondly, it is precisely because it *is* the employer's *business* that an employer can and should be concerned about employee substance abuse and its impact. It is the employer's ultimate responsibility to assure that the business is run safely, profitably, and productively. Drug abuse by employees does affect the workplace directly and substantially. This has been documented time and time again.

For example, a study of those employees seeking help on the "cocaine hotline" found that:

- 75 percent said they had used drugs on the job,
- 64 percent admitted that drugs had adversely affected their job performance,
- 44 percent said they had *sold* drugs to other employees, and
- 18 percent said they had *stolen* from co-workers to support their habits.

Another study reported by the U.S. government found that those who illicitly used drugs were:

- 2.5 times more likely to have absences of eight days or more,
- 3.6 times more likely to injure themselves or another person in a workplace accident,
- 5 times more likely to be injured in an accident off the job which, in turn, affects attendance or performance on the job, and

• 5 times more likely to file a workers' compensation claim.

Furthermore, drug users who are employed are one-third *less* productive and incur 300 percent *higher* medical costs.

The Path of Addiction

But don't many people use drugs without losing control?

Some do—at least for a time. However, a drug abuser can be like a time bomb waiting to explode.

No one starts as an addict (or an alcoholic) or intends to become one. The so-called "recreational" drug users comprise the pool from which chronic drug abusers and drug addicts develop. Moreover, the psychology of addiction is such that it includes a process of denial; addicts very seldom admit their addiction voluntarily. The regression from casual to chronic user is veiled in denial.

Furthermore, even a "casual" user can present a substantial safety and health risk on the job to themselves, their co-workers, and the company's customers.

Additionally, there often is a "gateway" effect: use of less serious drugs often can lead to the use of more serious drugs; sporadic use can develop into chronic use; and people, well-intentioned people, people who never considered addiction a possibility, can become desperate addicts, stealing and dealing to support their habits, and sometimes dying the tragic death of an addict.

Workplace Crime

What about crime on the job?

Drug abuse has a *major* impact on workplace crime. If you have a $3,000-a-month narcotic habit—which some people do—chances are you do not support that habit with just your paycheck. Drug addiction is a major cause of embezzlement and other employee thefts from U.S. companies.

Drug abuse and the obsession with the next "hit"—and how to pay for it—also compromise the workplace through stealing from co-workers, the potential for blackmail, ties to organized crime, and the violence associated with drug dealing.

As was mentioned earlier, 66 percent of those engaged in illicit drug use are employed. *Most* get their drugs from co-workers, on or off the job. The workplace often provides the perfect cover for buying and selling drugs.

In fact, treatment professionals tell us that the job is the last thing to go—first, because of denial ("I can't have a drug problem, I'm still working, aren't I?"); second, because the drug abuser needs the paycheck to pay for drugs; and third, because the workplace provides the opportunity for stealing and dealing that the addict often desperately needs.

> *"Drug users who are employed are one-third less productive and incur 300 percent higher medical costs."*

How prevalent is this problem in the workplace?

Between 500 and 600 employees at General Motors already have been arrested on the job for drug dealing.

Furthermore, it also is important to recognize *how* the workplace is compromised by drug dealing: the introduction of the criminal element; dealer-employees carrying weapons and large amounts of cash, protecting their turf in what, overall, is a $110-billion-a-year underground drug economy; and the threat this poses to supervisors and co-workers who stand in the way.

> *"If you have drug **users** in your company, you probably have drug **dealers** in your company."*

If you have drug *users* in your company, you probably have drug *dealers* in your company. . . .

The Danger of Marijuana

Yes, cocaine is serious, but just how dangerous can marijuana really be?

Very dangerous. As was mentioned earlier, marijuana today can have 22 times the potency (THC content) that marijuana did in the late '60s.

Moreover, marijuana can be a highly addictive drug. It is retained in the fatty tissue of the body for several days and it can cause impairment long after the "high" wears off.

A study at Stanford University in which airline pilots smoked relatively weak government-issued marijuana cigarettes, and then were tested on computerized flight simulators, predictably resulted in "crashes" right after the marijuana use. More alarming, however, was the fact that it also resulted in "crashes" 24 hours later when every pilot reported no residual effects and no reservations about "flying."

Finally, an incident at American Airlines dramatically demonstrates marijuana's potential impact on the workplace. One computer operator—high on marijuana while working at the airline's central reservations system—failed to load a tape in the computer at a critical juncture. The result: eight hours of down time for the entire reservations system, significant erasures, and a $19 million loss for the airline.

Many people would say airlines should be concerned about their pilots' or mechanics' drug use, but not necessarily about such use among their reservations personnel. Many would say employers have a legitimate interest in preventing employee abuse of "crack" or "ice," but not a "soft drug" like marijuana.

Chances are there is at least one airline which disagrees. . . .

Employees Favor Drug Testing

What are employees' views?

Provided drug testing is done with appropriate procedural safeguards, is consistently enforced, and is conducted pursuant to a policy that is well-communicated, it usually is well-received by employees.

In fact, a national Gallup survey of employees demonstrated an increasing in-tolerance among employees for drug abuse and drug abusers, and an accep-tance—if not an expectation—that employers take strong steps to provide drug-free workplaces.

When asked, "What is the greatest problem facing the United States today?", 28 percent of employees responding to the national Gallup survey answered "drugs," the most common answer and the response given more than two-and-a-half times more frequently than the second most common answer.

Of those employees whose companies do *not* have a drug testing program, nearly two-thirds (66 percent) would favor their company implementing drug testing, while only 26 percent would oppose it.

Of the 59 percent of employees whose companies have *policies* against drug abuse, 22 percent feel it is "not strong enough"; only 2 percent said it is "too strong."

Perhaps most telling, more than 97 percent of employees favor drug testing in the workplace at least under some circumstances.

Most workers are not drug abusers, do not want to work side-by-side with drug abusers and, in fact, are parents concerned about their kids' exposure to drugs as well.

The bottom line is: employees and employers are on the same side in the "war on drugs," and that side is decisively in favor of a strong anti-drug abuse com-pany policy and enforcement of that policy. Drug abuse in the workplace is not a labor-management *problem,* so much as it is a common *concern* of employees and employers.

Everyone Is Affected

But does drug abuse really affect me?

It affects *all* of us *as citizens:* higher taxes, higher insurance rates, more crime, higher health care costs, and higher prices. In fact, the cost of your car may have been as much as $430 more because of the drug abusers who work—or worked—at the plant where your car was made.

But it also affects *most* of us *as employees.* As was mentioned earlier, a drug abuser: (1) is 3.6 times more likely to cause a workplace accident, a sig-nificant safety risk; (2) is one-third less productive, thereby affecting the company's competitiveness and prof-itability (and devaluing employees' company stock and profit-sharing, as well as increasing the likelihood of layoffs); and (3) incurs 300 percent higher health care costs.

> *"More than 97 percent of employees favor drug testing in the workplace at least under some circumstances."*

A major telecommunications company reports that *40 percent* of its health care costs are attributable to substance abuse.

The next time your co-payments or deductibles go up, medical coverage is scaled back, or your monthly deductions are increased, you may wish to thank the drug abusers in your company. Not only may they be counterproductive and a serious safety risk, they may be taking money out of your pocket.

Do company programs work?

They do, if they are done "right" and accepted by the work force.

First of all, drug testing works. It's that simple. Some drug users don't even apply, some stop using for fear of being caught, and some are caught and go straight.

There are numerous success stories in both the private and public sectors, but perhaps none as dramatic as the U.S. Navy's: a decrease from 48 to 4 percent of its sailors engaged in illicit drug use in the '80s due to the implementation of a comprehensive drug abuse prevention program—including drug testing.

Moreover, company-provided employee assistance programs *save lives.* The lowest recidivism rates for drug abusers enrolled in treatment are among company-referred patients. Why?—because typically the most effective company EAPs provide: (1) support groups within the company, (2) counseling for family members, and most importantly, (3) the promise of a job waiting for those who successfully complete treatment. Company-sponsored rehabilitation is responsible, humane, and—for many—it works. For those who are unwilling or unable to complete rehabilitation, at least their psychology of denial is broken.

> *"The lowest recidivism rates for drug abusers enrolled in treatment are among company-referred patients."*

Federal Arrestees Should Be Tested for Drugs

by Bill Clinton and Janet Reno

About the authors: *Bill Clinton was elected the forty-second U.S. president in 1992 and reelected in 1996. He appointed Janet Reno as attorney general of the United States in 1993.*

Editor's note: The following statements were given at a press conference on December 18, 1995, the day Bill Clinton signed a presidential directive calling for drug testing of federal arrestees.

Bill Clinton: The criminal justice systems of our country are overburdened with drug-abusing defendants who cycle through the system while continuing to use drugs. Far too many criminals brought into our system have a substance abuse problem. In fact, a 1993 study by the Justice Department found that more than half of the arrestees tested positive for an illicit substance. Unless we break the cycle of drugs and crime, criminal addicts will end up back on the street, committing more crimes, and then right back in the criminal justice system still hooked on drugs. That's not fair to the taxpayers, the crime victims, or the American public. The cycle must be broken.

Accepting Responsibility

All across our country employers have accepted responsibility to reduce the level of drug use in the workplace. Teachers and coaches have accepted the responsibility to reduce the level of drug use in our schools. Now it is time for agencies in our criminal justice system to use all their power to reduce drug use by federal arrestees.

With this directive, when you enter the federal criminal justice system, you will be tested. If you have been taking drugs you should suffer the consequences. The administration is committed to breaking this link between crime and drugs. Indeed, if we could break it we could dramatically lower the crime rate.

From Bill Clinton and Janet Reno, "Remarks by the President on the President's Directive on Drug Testing," press release, December 18, 1995.

As a nation, there is only one message we can send: Continued drug use is unacceptable. We can't have a comprehensive crime-fighting effort until we end drug offenders' habits. That's why it's critical that the criminal justice system put all its power behind cleaning up drug-abusing criminals.

This directive is another example in which the federal criminal justice system can serve as a model for states. I'm very honored to be joined by the Minnesota Attorney General, Mr. Skip Humphrey, and the District Attorneys of Philadelphia and South Bend, Indiana. When they leave here today they're going home to ask their state legislatures to follow our lead in making sure all offenders are drug-tested. I call upon every governor, every state assembly, every state attorney general to do the same.

> *"We can't tolerate a revolving door of criminal drug abusers in our system."*

I'm proud of our antidrug strategy. It combines tough enforcement with a real, comprehensive prevention program and more investment in treatment. This directive is another step in our efforts to eliminate illegal drug use.

We know that reducing drug use will require everyone's effort. That's why [former] Drug Director Dr. Lee Brown [went to] California urging high school coaches to adopt drug testing of their athletes in order to reduce drug use among our teenagers.

Intolerance of Drug Abuse and Crime

These two actions send a clear and unambiguous message: Drug use and drug abuse are both wrong and illegal. We can't tolerate a revolving door of criminal drug abusers in our system. And if we work together, we can ensure that all the offenders in our country become drug-free and stay drug-free if they're going to stay out of jail.

Just yesterday, the FBI reported that for the first six months of 1995, violent crime was down by five percent and the murder rate was down by 12 percent. Over the last three years, we've made "three strikes and you're out" the law of the land, passed the Brady Bill [regulating handgun sales], the assault weapons ban. We're well on our way to putting those 100,000 new police officers on the American streets. But there is still one very disturbing and unacceptable finding in the FBI report, the trend of violence being committed by juveniles.

Later this week, I will be sending the Enhanced Prosecution of Dangerous Juvenile Offenders Act to the Congress. This legislation will help to address the critical problem of youth criminals by strengthening federal laws designed to deal with genuinely violent use. [As of June 1997, the bill had not come to a vote.] It's an additional tool for prosecutors to deal with violent juvenile criminals by holding dangerous youth criminals accountable for their actions. Once they've been arrested we must stop them from repeating their crimes.

With these steps that we've announced today, federal arrestees who are abusing drugs will no longer be out on the streets, and hardened criminals will be dealt with accordingly, even if they're juveniles.

Questions of Constitutionality

Q: Do you think that's constitutional?

Clinton: The way it is drawn, I do. The Attorney General might want to explain it, but, basically, in the places where this has been tried the people who are arrested are asked to undergo drug testing. As I understand it, about 80 percent of them agree. If they don't agree, instead of being forced it's just reported to the judge in making a determination about how high to set bail and what the conditions of bail should be.

Q: Well, if they are found to have taken drugs, does this mean they're not eligible for bail?

Clinton: Well, it means it can change the circumstances under which they're tried and what they might have to do as a condition.

Janet Reno: What it is saying—it is clearly constitutional to condition bail on testing. And what this says is if you are going to get bail you may have to agree to testing, you may have to agree to continued testing, to supervision, to certain conduct while you're on bail. Or it may mean that you have got to remain in the jail because the conditions would not ensure that you would be drug-free once you were on the streets.

Q: Wouldn't you be subject to additional charges, though? You know, in other words, you're arrested on some totally unrelated charge and you're found to have had drugs.

Reno: What we're trying to do is to prevent the unrelated charge that hap-

> *"We're going to try to do everything we can to ensure the safety of our streets based on these offenders and their condition."*

pens once they've left the courthouse. And if they are using drugs and if drugs are what is fueling so much of crime in this country, to send them back out without doing something to interrupt that cycle and to let a crime happen that was drug-induced doesn't make any sense.

What the President is doing here is saying, look, we're going to try to do everything we can to ensure the safety of our streets based on these offenders and their condition, and we're also going to try to do something to make sure that we interrupt the cycle of drug use on the part of these offenders.

Workplace Drug Testing Is Ineffective and Unfair

by American Civil Liberties Union

About the author: *The American Civil Liberties Union (ACLU) is a New York City organization that champions the human rights set forth in the Declaration of Independence and the Constitution. It has many local chapters across the United States.*

Today, in some industries, taking a drug test is as routine as filling out a job application.

In fact, workplace drug testing is up 277 percent from 1987—despite the fact that random drug testing is unfair, often inaccurate and unproven as a means of stopping drug use.

But because there are few laws protecting our privacy in the workplace, millions of American workers are tested yearly—even though they aren't suspected of drug use.

Employers have the right to expect workers not to be high or drunk on the job. But they shouldn't have the right to require employees to prove their innocence by taking a drug test.

That's not how America should work.

Invasion and Error

However routine drug tests have become, they're still intrusive. Often, another person is there to observe the employee to ensure there is no specimen tampering. Even indirect observation can be degrading; typically, workers must remove their outer garments and urinate in a bathroom in which the water supply has been turned off.

The lab procedure is a second invasion of privacy. Urinalysis reveals not only the presence of illegal drugs, but also the existence of many other physical and medical conditions, including genetic predisposition to disease—or pregnancy. In 1988, the Washington, D.C., Police Department admitted it used urine samples collected for drug tests to screen female employees for pregnancy—*with-*

From the American Civil Liberties Union, *In Brief*, "Privacy in America: Workplace Drug Testing," 1996. Reprinted by permission of the ACLU.

out their knowledge or consent.

Furthermore, human error in the lab, or the test's failure to distinguish between legal and illegal substances, can make even a small margin of error add up to a huge potential for false positive results. In 1992, an estimated 22 million tests were administered. If five percent yielded false positive results (a conservative estimate of false positive rates) that means 1.1 million people who could have been fired, or denied jobs, because of a mistake.

Tests That Fail

Claims of billions of dollars lost in employee productivity are based on guesswork, not real evidence.

Drug abuse in the workplace affects a relatively small percentage of workers. A 1994 National Academy of Sciences report found workplace drug use "ranges from a modest to a moderate extent," and noted that much of reported drug use "may be single incident, perhaps even at events like office parties."

> *"Millions of American workers are tested yearly— even though they aren't suspected of drug use."*

Furthermore, drug tests are not work-related because they do not measure on-the-job impairment. A positive drug test only reveals that a drug was ingested at some time in the past. Nor do they distinguish between occasional and habitual use.

Drug testing is designed to detect and punish conduct that is usually engaged in off-duty and off the employer's premises—that is, in private. Employers who conduct random drug tests on workers who are not suspected of using drugs are policing private behavior that has no impact on job performance.

About Safety-Sensitive Occupations

Alertness and sobriety are, of course, imperative for certain occupations, such as train engineers, airline pilots, truck drivers and others. Yet even in these jobs, random drug testing does not guarantee safety. Firstly, drug-related employee impairment in safety-sensitive jobs is rare. There has never been a commercial airline accident linked to pilot drug use. And even after a 1994 Amtrak accident in which several lives were lost, investigators discovered the train engineer had a well-known history of alcohol, not drug, abuse.

Computer-assisted performance tests, which measure hand-eye coordination and response time, are a better way of detecting whether employees are up to the job. NASA, for example, has long used task-performance tests to determine whether astronauts and pilots are unfit for work—whether the cause is substance abuse, fatigue, or physical illness.

Drug tests don't prevent accidents because they don't address the root problems that lead to substance abuse. But good management and counseling can.

Employee assistance programs (EAPs) help people facing emotional, health, financial or substance abuse problems that can affect job performance. EAP counselors decide what type of help is needed: staff support, inpatient treatment, AA meetings, and the like. In this context, the goal is rehabilitation and wellness—not punishment.

Employers need to kick the drug test habit.

Privacy Rights

Privacy—the right to be left alone—is one of our most cherished rights. Yet because so few laws protect our privacy, the ACLU's campaign for privacy in the workplace is very important—particularly in the private sector.

The ACLU is working in the states to help enact legislation to protect workplace privacy rights. We have created a model statute regulating workplace drug testing. In 1996 the ACLU launched a public education campaign to help individuals across the nation become aware of the need for increased workplace privacy rights. Our educational videotape *Through the Keyhole: Privacy in the Workplace—An Endangered Right* was featured on national television and at union meetings and other gatherings nationwide.

Much more work remains to be done. As of mid-1997, only a handful of states ban testing that is not based on individual suspicion: Montana, Iowa, Vermont, and Rhode Island. Minnesota, Maine, and Connecticut permit not-for-cause testing, but only of employees in safety-sensitive positions. These laws also require confirmation testing, lab certification, and test result confidentiality.

Hawaii, Louisiana, Maryland, Nebraska, Oregon, and Utah regulate drug testing in some fashion; Florida and Kansas protect government employee rights, but not those of private sector workers. Only in California, Massachusetts, and New Jersey have

"Drug tests don't prevent accidents because they don't address the root problems that lead to substance abuse."

the highest courts ruled out some forms of drug testing on state constitutional or statutory grounds. The ACLU is now continuing our efforts to protect workplace privacy rights.

Random Drug Tests Do Not Ensure a Drug-Free Workplace

by National Organization for the Reform of Marijuana Laws

About the author: *The Washington, D.C.–based National Organization for the Reform of Marijuana Laws (NORML) advocates the legalization of marijuana.*

> The right of the people to be secure in their persons . . . against unreasonable searches and seizures, shall not be violated, and no Warrants shall issue, but upon probable cause.
>
> —The Fourth Amendment to the United States Constitution

> We would be appalled at the spectre of the police spying on employees during their free time and then reporting their activities to their employers. Drug testing is a form of surveillance, albeit a technological one. Nonetheless, it reports on a person's off-duty activities just as surely as if someone had been present and watching. It is George Orwell's Big Brother Society come to life.
>
> —Federal Judge H. Lee Sarokin, September 18, 1986

Employees now entering the work force can expect to undergo 10 to 100 tests for off-the-job drug consumption during their careers. Asked to "prove" their innocence in exchange for job security, these workers will stand accused without evidence or even suspicion.

On March 21, 1989, the U.S. Supreme Court handed down its first ruling on the constitutionality of testing employees who are not actually suspected of consuming drugs, authorizing the suspicionless testing of millions of government workers. Drug testing is being touted as a panacea for all workplace problems. The millions of workers who are subjected to these intrusive, degrading tests know better than anyone: Drug testing does not work, and it is making a mockery of the United States Constitution.

Drug testing has overridden the Constitution.

The U.S. Supreme Court has ruled that even though drug tests are searches

Reprinted by permission from the online version of NORML's 1995 brochure *Drug Testing for Work* at www.natlnorml.org/testing/flyer.shtml.

that must comply with the Fourth Amendment's "reasonableness" requirement, there are instances of "special needs" in which individuals may be subjected to suspicionless, warrantless searches. In these cases, the workers' constitutionally guaranteed right to privacy is outweighed by the government's interest in maintaining a drug-free workplace.

In the words of dissenting Justice Thurgood Marshall, the 1989 ruling left the Fourth Amendment "devoid of meaning, subject to whatever content shifting majorities concerned about the problems of the day choose to give that supple term ['special needs']."

Drug testing denies private workers the protection afforded to public workers.

> *"Lower courts have struck down as unconstitutional the random testing of police officers, teachers, [and] fire fighters."*

While the U.S. Supreme Court has allowed the drug testing of millions of public workers in positions deemed "safety-sensitive" or "security-sensitive," lower courts have struck down as unconstitutional the random testing of police officers, teachers, fire fighters, prison guards, civilian army employees, and employees of many federal agencies.

However, because the Constitution only protects citizens from the government and not from private individuals or companies, private sector employees in comparable positions are not afforded these same guarantees. In most states, private sector employees have virtually no protection against drug testing's intrusion on their privacy. Nevertheless, it is abhorrent that private employers are subjecting their workers to drug tests under circumstances that the government does not recognize as justifiable grounds for testing its employees.

False Positive Tests

Drug testing is inaccurate and unreliable.

Contrary to what companies that test would have us believe, drug tests are not foolproof. In fact, only 85 of the estimated 1,200 laboratories in the United States currently testing urine for drugs meet federal standards for accuracy, qualified lab personnel, and proper documentation and record-keeping procedures. Because private companies are not required to use certified labs, workers are being asked to put their job security in the hands of a test that has insufficient quality controls. Even in labs that do meet the minimum standards, there is plenty of room for error. The sample passes through many hands as it goes from collection to final analysis, and a single human error can cause a specimen to be mistakenly identified as positive ("false positive").

Hair tests, while much less common than urinalysis, are being administered with increasing frequency and have a whole set of other problems. Environmental contaminants such as smoke can enter the hair follicle, resulting in a positive test for someone who has simply been in a room in which drugs were being smoked. Non-Caucasian hair seems to absorb more drug residue than Caucasian hair, resulting in an obvious racial bias. The federal government has refused to certify any hair analysis labs because of the troublesome questions that still persist about their accuracy.

Blood tests, the most accurate of tests, are rarely used because drawing blood is considered too invasive.

False positives also can be caused by glitches in the testing technology. In a notorious 1984 incident, 60,000 Army personnel were informed that their tests had been wrong. Today, the most conservative estimates of the number of false positives per year run into the thousands. In fact, the highest estimate of accuracy reported to date shows one false positive in every 700 samples. Considering the number of times workers are tested, as many as 1 in every 15 workers can expect to have a false positive at some point in his or her career.

Hundreds of thousands of American citizens are having their livelihoods jeopardized by a test that is of dubious accuracy at best.

What Drug Tests Do Not Detect

Random drug testing does not ensure a drug-free workplace.

Employers have the right to want a safe and productive workplace. Randomly administered drug tests, however, do nothing to further this goal and can actually hinder it.

Overlooked in the debate about drug testing is the fact that drug testing has never been scientifically shown to improve workplace safety or productivity. This is most likely because drug tests do not measure current impairment. They can only determine whether metabolites from past drug use are present in the medium being tested. For instance, metabolites from marijuana consumption can be detected in the urine for more than 30 days after the person's last exposure to marijuana. Obviously, a drug test will not distinguish between on-the-job use and private consumption. And because marijuana consumption is detectable for much longer than for any other drug, a worker who consumed marijuana one month earlier—on the weekend—could test positive while someone who used cocaine three days earlier—on the job—could test negative.

Hair testing is even more bizarre. A hair test can detect past drug consumption as far as several years back if the hair is long enough. It is difficult to imagine what possible legitimate use an employer would have for such information.

> *"Hundreds of thousands of American citizens are having their livelihoods jeopardized by a test that is of dubious accuracy at best."*

Drug tests do not detect alcohol, our nation's leading drug of abuse. Tests that do detect alcohol are separate, rarely administered, and only detect current impairment. Drug tests do not detect fatigue or stress, the cause of one-third of all workplace accidents. They assess nothing except how the employee lives his or her private life. In light of this, it is not surprising that most studies find no correlation between test result and job performance. Additionally, with 70% of all drug consumers employed, it is difficult to argue that the choice to consume drugs off the job makes one unfit to work.

> *"Drug testing has reached endemic proportions not because it improves the workplace but because it penalizes the casual drug consumer."*

In fact, the much-publicized claims that drug consumption costs businesses billions of dollars in lost productivity and accidents are all based on a single study which the federal government has since found to be flawed.

Plainly put, drug tests have nothing to do with safety or productivity. What they are about is ensuring a drug-free workforce, not the drug-free workplace touted as the goal. Whether individual employers realize it or not, drug testing has reached endemic proportions not because it improves the workplace but because it penalizes the casual drug consumer—someone who might not suffer any consequences from his or her drug consumption otherwise. The White House's 1989 National Drug Control Strategy clearly states: "The non-addicted casual or regular user . . . is likely to have a still-intact family, social, and work life. . . . [They] now avoid any penalty whatsoever. . . . *Businesses and employers must make it clear that drug use and employment are incompatible.*" (emphasis added) The report goes on to encourage employers to institute drug testing programs for all employees. Drug tests in the workplace are nothing more than the government's attempt to manufacture negative consequences for drug consumers who otherwise might encounter none.

A Violation of Rights

Drug tests violate workers' rights.

Drug tests violate the constitutional guarantee of presumption of innocence, placing the burden of proof on the accused. (Most drug tests are administered not to those suspected of drug use, but to all workers in the office on a random basis.) By being required to give a sample, the worker is forced to defend himself or herself against a charge without any evidence or suspicion. American workers are now treated as guilty until proven innocent.

Drug tests can reveal private details far beyond what substances a person chooses to ingest. For instance, a drug test can reveal if the employee is receiving treatment for epilepsy, depression, or AIDS. Urinalysis can also reveal if a female employee is pregnant. It is illegal to require employees to provide such information in written or verbal form—so why can employers scrutinize their bodily fluids? Drug testing as described in the 1987 case of *Jones v. McKenzie*, can "provide employers with a periscope through which they can peer into an individual's behavior in her private life, even in her own home. . . ."

Drug tests have detrimental impact on the workplace.

Not only do drug tests not accomplish what they are intended to do, but they actually exercise a negative effect on the workplace by decreasing worker morale, wasting huge sums of money, and taking the focus off of employee performance.

Drug testing sends the message to employees that the merit of their work can always be eclipsed by whatever chemical residue is detected in their urine on any given day. It forces workers to live in fear, never completely secure in their jobs, always at the mercy of the accuracy of the tests. It fosters an atmosphere of distrust as employees are forced to prove their "innocence" over and over again.

A False Sense of Security

Drug testing sends worker morale plummeting, as many workers resent the monitoring of off-the-job activities that do not affect on-the-job performance. Perversely, drug testing also can encourage employees to move away from soft drugs like marijuana—which remains detectable longer than any other substance—toward harder drugs like cocaine and heroin, both of which are undetectable after 2 to 3 days.

Meanwhile, drug testing encourages a false sense of security in employers and supervisors who are led to believe that workers who test negative must be free from substance-related problems. In fact, 1 in every 10 Americans has an alcohol problem—a problem that a drug test will not detect.

Private and public employers spend $1.2 billion on drug testing annually. For every $40,000 spent on drug testing, only one employee is correctly identified as a drug consumer. Even if drug tests were accurate—which they are not—it would be difficult to justify such a price.

Employers are paying exorbitant prices to recreate a technologized version of the past, when employers could hire or fire based on their employees' family life, sexual habits, and choice of associates.

Performance Tests

An alternative to drug testing exists.

For decades, tests known as performance or impairment tests have been providing enlightened employers with a reliable, cost-effective way to test the functional capacity of employees without invading privacy. Impairment tests are computer-based, employee-operated tests that measure hand-eye coordination, visual tracking ability, and basic cognitive skills.

> *"Drug testing encourages a false sense of security in employers and supervisors."*

They can be used daily or immediately before a worker is about to perform a safety-sensitive duty, and they provide immediate feedback, unlike drug tests, when days and even weeks can go by before test results are known.

Use of these tests has lowered accidents by as much as 67% in the businesses that have implemented them. Workplace errors have been reduced by over 50%. Focusing solely on performance, impairment tests detect impairment not only from drug consumption, but also from fatigue, emotional stress, legal drugs such as alcohol and antihistamines, and undiagnosed medical conditions.

Impairment tests accomplish what drug tests are purported to do—without violating workers' rights.

Drug Testing of Federal Arrestees Is Unconstitutional

by National Association of Criminal Defense Lawyers

About the author: *The National Association of Criminal Defense Lawyers is a membership organization located in Washington, D.C.*

In December 1995, President Bill Clinton announced by "Executive Order" that through his administrative agencies, all persons arrested on federal criminal charges (*any and all charges*) would forthwith be required to submit to drug tests as a "condition" of release from agency custody on bail. When formally directing the executive branch in the fulfillment of a particular program, the President may implement his authority through an executive order. Presidents traditionally have used these orders to implement their "*most important initiatives,* basing them on any combination of constitutional and statutory authority that is thought to be available," according to Peter M. Shane and Harold H. Bruff (emphasis added here). Thus, these orders often dwell in a constitutional place Justice Robert H. Jackson termed a "zone of twilight," where presidential authority (*vis a vis* the other branches of government, and *vis a vis* individual rights and liberties) is neither clearly present nor absent. Executive orders are best understood as "presidential legislation."

The Power of "Presidential Legislation"

Unfortunately, even "presidential legislation" lacking in authority can gain a foothold over fundamental individual freedom when Congress fails over time to step in and stop its wrongful effectuation. Right or wrong, when a president's view of his own authority has been acted upon over a substantial period of time without eliciting congressional reversal, it is frequently held by the third branch of government, the judiciary, to be "entitled to great respect."

This new national policy would apply to persons arrested for crimes that have

Reprinted by permission from the National Association of Criminal Defense Lawyers, October 1996 position paper, "Unconstitutional 'Conditioning' of Citizen Freedom: Drug Tests for Bail; Big Brother for Public Housing," at www.criminaljustice.org/LEGIS/leg19.htm.

nothing to do with drugs. In an Orwellian "fishing expedition" through citizen privacy, abortion protesters, business people charged with violating complicated regulatory or tax requirements, elected officials charged with failing to comply with financial disclosure requirements or statutory prohibitions on receiving gifts, all would have to submit to drug tests upon arrest if they hope to be freed while the cases against them proceed. *Or would they?* Would the test-searches be deployed only in the most arbitrary, "selective" fashion, against the most vulnerable citizens, or those "suspected" of drug use, by

> *"The Clinton drug testing order flies in the face of several sacred constitutional provisions for citizen rights and liberties."*

those wielding the discretionary power of the test? Under either practical scenario, this unreasonable, inherently coercive and intrusive search and seizure tool is an unconstitutional one. Congress and the courts should reject this offensive "presidential legislation" immediately, lest it gain a dangerous foothold over citizen freedom.

The Clinton drug testing order flies in the face of several sacred constitutional provisions for citizen rights and liberties. It is fundamental to our system of constitutional democracy that "the integrity of an individual's person is a cherished value of our society," as stated in *Schmerber v. California* (1966). And the bodily "fishing expedition" by the government threatened by the executive order is forbidden.

The Fourth Amendment and the Right to Privacy

For instance, the Fourth Amendment, and the recognized broader right to privacy, guarantee the right of the people to be secure in their persons from unreasonable searches, seizures, and other encroachments upon personal integrity. The mere fact of some lawful arrest of a person does not end the inquiry. The interests in human dignity which the Fourth Amendment and the right to privacy protect forbid intrusions like those contemplated by the Clinton drug-testing executive order—that is, those resting upon a mere suspicion or chance that desired evidence of drug criminality might be obtained. Certainly, in the absence of a clear indication (probable cause) that such will be found, and some emergency circumstance, these fundamental human interests of dignity and privacy require law officers (including probation officers) to "suffer the risk that such evidence may disappear unless there is an immediate search," according to *Schmerber*. See also *Winston v. Lee* (1985) ("A compelled surgical intrusion into an individual's body for evidence . . . implicates expectations of privacy and security of such magnitude that the intrusion may be 'unreasonable' even if likely to produce evidence of a crime").

The executive order also violates the Eighth Amendment, which generally guarantees bail for persons detained by the government. And it lacks any plau-

sible connection (necessary nexus, or *germainess*) to the legitimate goals of ac-
tual statutory authority on which it might purportedly be based, and so violates
fundamental due process under the Fifth Amendment, as well.

Presumed Innocent

Arrested persons are presumed innocent, and the Eighth Amendment and Due
Process generally gives them a right to be freed pending trial. *The only excep-*
tions approved by courts in over 200 years are:

- if the court finds a defendant is likely to flee the jurisdiction prior to trial,
  regardless of how high bail is set; or
- under the Bail Reform Act of 1984, if a court finds the defendant may well
  pose a danger to the community if released.

In signing an executive order instructing the Attorney General to design a
plan for implementation of this "test-them-all" policy, the President should
have known (or been advised by learned counsel) that neither he nor the Attorney General actually had the legal authority to deny freedom on bail to persons
arrested on federal charges because of their refusal to take drug tests—that this
is an unconstitutional "conditioning" (governmental hostage-taking) of citizen
rights. As the President and Attorney General must know, their policy will in
practice require federal prosecutors to:

- "request" (read coerce) every person arrested on federal charges to take a
  drug test;
- raise the defendant's refusal to take a drug test, or raise the results of a drug
  test, to the court as an issue at the bail hearing;
- ask the court to deny release on bail to defendants who refuse to take drug
  tests; and
- recommend to the court that conditions be set for release of defendants who
  test positive for drugs.

The reality is that arrest and detention by federal law enforcement authorities
is a frightening, intimidating, and inherently coercive situation. Arrested individuals who are approached with a "request" by a federal agent or prosecutor to
take a drug test are unlikely to feel free to refuse. When they are informed that
they may be denied their freedom un-
less they take the test, the likelihood
of their refusing diminishes even further. Thus, "requesting" that defendants submit to drug test-searches,
with the threat of continued imprisonment prior to trial hanging over
their heads, effectively nullifies their

> *"Arrested persons are*
> *presumed innocent, and the*
> *Eighth Amendment and Due*
> *Process generally gives them a*
> *right to be freed pending trial."*

Fourth Amendment, Eighth Amendment, due process and privacy rights.

U.S. Attorneys have no right to make one's willingness to submit to a drug
test-search a condition of release or an "issue" at a bail hearing. There is no

room in American law for prolonging detention as a "penalty" for not taking a drug test.

Even as a matter of mere pragmatics, there is no room in America's already over-burdened courts for this presidential legislation: how are they supposed to oversee the bureaucratic administration of this type of policy? How many "false positive" cases are they going to have to contend with, in which citizens raise valid claims that they have been victimized not only by the administration's unconstitutional policy generally, but that false testing results have resulted in the deprivation of their rights and liberties. Such false positive cases are already an established legal phenomenon in other testing contexts in which false results have robbed an individual of his or her rightful interests.

> *"U.S. Attorneys have no right to make one's willingness to submit to a drug test-search a condition of release or an 'issue' at a bail hearing."*

Coercing the States

Moreover, the President expressly directed the Attorney General to "take all appropriate steps to encourage the states to implement the same policies." As happens all too often in other areas, the federal government would use financial and other pressures to coerce state governments to make drug testing a condition of freedom for defendants. As states begin to fall into line with the President's "request," any suspected criminal anywhere will be required to submit to a privacy-invading, humiliating drug test before regaining his or her freedom. This is Big Brother writ large, violative of all the above-referenced, individual constitutional rights and liberties in addition to the *Fourteenth Amendment*, which secures the citizen against state invasions of the same privileges secured against *federal* infringement by the right to privacy and the Fourth, Fifth, and Eighth Amendments.

Chapter 3

Are Antidrug Programs Effective?

Chapter Preface

In 1983, the Los Angeles Police Department created the D.A.R.E. (Drug Abuse Resistance Education) program to encourage youths to avoid illegal drugs. Today D.A.R.E., which is taught by police officers (primarily to fifth- and sixth-graders) in half of the nation's school districts, is America's most prominent school drug-education program.

Advocates of D.A.R.E. credit the program not only for warning children about the dangers of drug use, but for improving youths' self-esteem and decision-making skills. Robert E. Peterson, director of Michigan's Office of Drug Control Policy, argues that although D.A.R.E. should not be considered a "magic bullet . . . to prevent drug use," the program "increases student and parent confidence that they can avoid drugs and deal with peer pressure."

However, many critics contend that there is no evidence that D.A.R.E. reduces drug abuse among students. These observers cite a 1994 U.S. Department of Justice–funded study that concluded that D.A.R.E. had no statistically significant impact in reducing drug use rates among D.A.R.E. participants. Anecdotal evidence supports this conclusion. According to one eighteen-year-old, "Mostly everyone I know who was in D.A.R.E. back with me are [smoking marijuana] and more. I don't think it worked. Not for me." Some school districts, such as Seattle's, have terminated D.A.R.E. because of unsatisfactory results.

Advocates of drug treatment and drug education programs assert that these methods can effectively reduce or prevent drug abuse. Critics disagree, arguing that such programs fail to convince individuals to avoid drugs or to break abusers' drug habits. In the following viewpoints, authors examine the effectiveness of D.A.R.E. and other antidrug programs.

The D.A.R.E. Program Is Effective

by Joseph F. Donnermeyer and G. Howard Phillips

About the authors: *Joseph F. Donnermeyer is an associate professor of agricultural education at Ohio State University in Columbus. G. Howard Phillips is a professor emeritus of agriculture at Ohio State University.*

Does D.A.R.E. make a difference in students' attitudes and behavior in the use of alcohol and drugs? To answer this question, 11th grade students were selected as the study population because they were old enough to have been confronted with opportunities to use alcohol, marijuana and hard drugs. Also, some students of this age would have had the opportunity to participate in the D.A.R.E. program at the elementary, junior high and senior high levels. Altogether, 3,150 11th grade students participated in this statewide assessment of D.A.R.E., funded by the Ohio Office of Criminal Justice Services. Results from this research showed that *D.A.R.E. does make a positive difference*.

The basic questionnaire consisted of a well-tested instrument developed by the American Drug and Alcohol Survey of the Rocky Mountain Behavioral Sciences Institute at Fort Collins, Colorado. More than 1,200 schools had previously used this instrument. A special insert was developed in order to examine issues pertinent to prevention education programs.

D.A.R.E. Students at Low Risk

Finding #1. Drug use among 11th grade students.

Students were classified into three risk groups. Low risk includes students who have never used drugs or alcohol, those who rarely drink, and those who had experimented with substances once or twice but not recently. Students who used alcohol on a more frequent basis, or used marijuana on an occasional, but not on a regular basis, were classified as moderate risk. Finally, high risk students were those who are heavy alcohol users or regular users of other drugs.

As shown in Table 1, students who had two or three D.A.R.E. classes (elementary, junior high and/or high school) were significantly more likely to be in

From Joseph F. Donnermeyer and G. Howard Phillips, "D.A.R.E. Works," research report, at http://www.dare-america.com/D_EDUC/DE_QUIC/DE_QUIC.HTM. Reprinted by permission of Dr. Donnermeyer.

the low risk group and conversely, less likely to be in the moderate and high risk categories. Students with only one exposure to D.A.R.E. were also more likely to be in the low risk group than students who had never attended D.A.R.E. classes. Students with no D.A.R.E. classes were less likely to be in the low risk group. In other words, they were more often in the higher risk groups. *These results strongly suggest D.A.R.E. does reduce substance use.*

> *"Students who had two or three D.A.R.E. classes . . . were significantly more likely to be in the low risk group."*

Table 1. Involvement in the D.A.R.E. Program

Level of Use of Alcohol and Other Drugs	D.A.R.E. Multiple Classes	D.A.R.E. Elementary	Non-D.A.R.E.
low risk	73%	63%*	58%*
moderate risk	17%	26%	28%
high risk	10%	12%	15%

*Percentages do not add up to 100% due to rounding.

D.A.R.E. and Peer Associations

Finding #2. Peer factors.

Research has shown that the most direct and influential link to alcohol and drug use among young people is the peer group, especially close friends. If adolescents associate with close peers who discourage substance use, they are much less likely to use alcohol and drugs themselves. If adolescents associate with close peers who encourage substance use, they are much more likely to use alcohol and drugs. D.A.R.E. strengthens peer associations that discourage substance use and increases resistance to peers who encourage it.

Table 2. Peer Associations and Substance Use

Friends would stop them from:	D.A.R.E.	Non-D.A.R.E.
getting drunk	21%	15%
using inhalants	66%	59%
using marijuana	43%	32%
using hard drugs	75%	68%

Would stop friends from using:	D.A.R.E.	Non-D.A.R.E.
marijuana	59%	44%
inhalants	82%	71%

Would say "no" to close friends who would ask them to:	D.A.R.E	Non-D.A.R.E.
get drunk	77%	66%
smoke cigarettes	80%	74%
use marijuana	84%	78%

Discussing Drugs

Finding #3. Learning about the dangers of drugs.

D.A.R.E. urges students to talk with their families about the dangers associated with different drugs. Eleventh graders with D.A.R.E. training were more likely to discuss these dangers with their parents than non-D.A.R.E. students.

Beyond parents and peers, students can learn about substances from other sources. As expected, D.A.R.E. officers were by far the primary source in D.A.R.E. schools. But the significant finding here is that students who had D.A.R.E. training more often sought out other school professionals for information about drugs and alcohol than non-D.A.R.E. students.

Effective in Many Ways

Finding #4. D.A.R.E. officers at school.

One of the additional benefits of the D.A.R.E. program is the opportunity for students to interact with police officers in a positive environment. D.A.R.E. officers spend additional time at the schools outside of the classroom to give students the opportunity to get to know them in a friendly, less formal way. A scale was devised to measure 11th graders' attitudes about police in two areas: respect for police, and whether or not they were viewed as helpful. Again, D.A.R.E. students saw police in a more positive light than students from non-D.A.R.E. schools.

This study found that D.A.R.E. did influence 11th grade students' attitudes and behaviors about substance use. The differences reported here were all statistically significant, and in a positive direction. All in all, D.A.R.E. reduced substance use, increased peer resistance, encouraged communication with parents and other responsible adults, and increased positive views of the police. Prevention education programs such as D.A.R.E. have a major role in teaching the dangers and consequences of substance abuse. Like other prevention efforts, D.A.R.E. plays an important role in supporting families, positive peer groups, and communities in order to raise healthy, responsible youth.

> *"D.A.R.E. strengthens peer associations that discourage substance use and increases resistance to peers who encourage it."*

Prison Drug Treatment Programs Are Effective

by Dan Weikel

About the author: *Dan Weikel is a* Los Angeles Times *staff writer.*

Capt. Michael Teischner was thrilled with his promotion at Donovan State Prison except for one thing. His new duties included supervising the facility's privately run drug treatment program.

Teischner—known as "Iceman" around the prison yard—didn't much believe in rehabilitating criminals. During his 20-year career with the California Department of Corrections, he had seen plenty of reform-minded do-gooders come and go.

When he met over lunch with Elaine Abraham of the nonprofit Amity Foundation, which runs the rehab center, he lived up to his moniker.

"Quite frankly," the Iceman said of prison treatment programs, "I don't think they work."

Years later, Teischner is a changed man—like many of the convicts who undergo Amity's yearlong regimen and now lead productive lives. Today, he says the only problem with drug and alcohol treatment is that the exploding prison population can't get enough of it.

A Powerful Weapon

Compared to the checkered performance of past substance abuse programs for convicts, Amity and similar projects around the country may offer corrections officials a powerful weapon to reduce crime, addiction and soaring prison costs.

Research shows that by weaning convicts off illegal drugs—which are widely available in prison—and overhauling their lifestyles, such programs can significantly lower re-incarceration rates, saving taxpayers millions of dollars a year.

Consequently, prison officials grappling with unprecedented overcrowding due to the nation's war on drugs have started to rethink how they deal with addicted prisoners. The task before them is daunting:

Nationally, only one in six of an estimated 800,000 inmates involved with illegal drugs receives any treatment, most of it sporadic education classes or weekly counseling sessions that don't do much good.

Little in the way of treatment has been provided because many law enforcement officials and legislators believe that tough sentences are the best way to deal with the nation's drug problem. Academic research in the mid-1970s also fostered the long-held, some say mistaken, belief that nothing works when it comes to reforming criminals.

> *"Such programs can significantly lower re-incarceration rates, saving taxpayers millions of dollars a year."*

In California, an estimated 100,000 state prison inmates have histories of chronic drug and alcohol use. But there are only 400 slots in the corrections system that offer treatment considered intensive enough to break the dangerous cycle of crime and addiction.

At Donovan, a medium security prison in an arid valley east of San Diego, hundreds of convicts apply for no more than 20 slots that become available every month. For those who get accepted, the treatment can rewire their lives.

The Amity Program

The Amity program, which opened at Donovan in 1990, contracts with the Corrections Department for $1.5 million a year. It is a so-called therapeutic community, a style of intensive residential treatment thought to be most effective for felons with substantial criminal records.

For nine to 12 months, 220 participants share a dormitory, dining facilities and recreation areas. Upon release from prison, graduating parolees can volunteer to continue taxpayer-funded counseling at Amity's residential off-site program nestled in a wooded hillside in north San Diego County.

At both facilities, convicts are required to attend a steady stream of seminars and encounter groups run by recovering addicts, ex-convicts and some of the most experienced substance abuse counselors in the field.

The routine is rigorous. No one gets time off their sentences for participating or reprieves from prison work. Unlike with rehabilitation efforts at other penitentiaries, Amity enrollees are not isolated from Donovan's main yard, where there are temptations to use smuggled drugs every day.

The goal is to teach convicts to deal with personal problems and to live life without drugs and crime.

But the job is difficult because inmates are among the hardest substance abusers to treat. Their complicated pathologies often include poverty, gang membership, mental illness and child abuse. Relapse is common, and change happens at a glacial pace over many months.

Much of the transformation, if it occurs, takes place in encounter groups that attempt to dissect—with brutal honesty—what caused the convict's substance abuse and criminal behavior.

The sessions are filled with discussions about trust, personal accountability, relationships with women, family problems, substance abuse and the inner rage that leads to violence. By drawing inmates out, counselors say, they can help them understand their problems and find solutions.

"Nothing Easy About Facing the Truth"

"There is nothing easy about facing the truth about yourself," former cocaine addict and crack dealer Terry Ward says of Amity's group discussions. "The badder you act the more they dig. It's hard to keep up the facade. They just pick pieces out of your story and make you humble. The first few months will tear you apart."

Ward, 40, was a violent hustler and convicted armed robber, known to the denizens of South-Central Los Angeles as "Voltron." He always carried two pistols, a knife and a cane that he used as a weapon.

Skilled with a razor blade, Ward could sculpt a $5 piece of crack so it looked like it was worth $15. On the street, he would not hesitate to beat up someone at the smallest provocation. He once broke a man's jaw for calling him by his given name.

Ward was paroled in 1991 after serving two years at Donovan. He stayed so long in Amity's off-site volunteer program that he had to be told to leave. Today, he manages a Wendy's restaurant and lives in Spring Valley, a rural community east of San Diego. He has finally gotten to know his 19-year-old daughter, whom he abandoned more than 10 years ago.

"The goal is to teach convicts to deal with personal problems and to live life without drugs and crime."

"Voltron was a bad person. He died in prison," Ward said. "There are people who go through Amity and use again. I choose not to. I've been insane long enough."

On one recent morning, 15 convicts, some just like Ward, gather for group therapy in the Robin Gabriel Room of Amity's prison compound. Gabriel graduated from an Amity jail program in Arizona, where the organization got its start in the 1980s. She devoted her life to the foundation until she died of cancer in 1990.

Half the people here are doing time for violent offenses, including murder. All have histories of drug and alcohol abuse. Though prison is a place where revealing inner feelings can be interpreted as a sign of weakness, most are not afraid to talk.

"All my relationships have been built on lies," says one barrel-chested convict with corn-rowed hair. "I fall in love with a woman and then she is with my best friend. Women just play a man's heart and throw 'em to the curb."

"I've never been around a decent woman," another inmate volunteers. "I've been in crack houses a lot of my life, and you don't trust anyone, man or woman."

"On the streets, I was a predator. I preyed on women," says counselor Ernie Logan, an ex-convict and recovering addict whose father was an alcoholic. "I had a lot of trust issues too. My mother and father betrayed me as a child."

Logan's reference to childhood strikes a chord with a goateed inmate sitting across from him. He is doing eight years for robbery. Rejection has weighed heavily on his mind for years.

"I'm very conscious of the pain I feel," he says. "If Ernie won't say hello to me, I feel like, '---- Ernie.' Something that small makes me think back on when I was a kid, all the shame and grief of being abandoned by my parents. That emotion has energy. The power is hard to control."

"But," counselor Logan responds, "if you are in touch with what happened to you and the pain it has caused you, you shouldn't be doing the same things to someone else. You shouldn't be taking it out on somebody else."

Treatment Is "Cheap and It Works"

If drug treatment advocates had their way, programs like Amity's would be available to every convict seeking help. Incarceration alone, they say, does not necessarily stop addiction or protect the public in the long run.

State figures show that the average drug offender in California, whether convicted of sales, distribution or possession, is returned to the street in 18 to 24 months.

Proponents say effective drug treatment programs can be provided at a fraction of the billions of dollars being spent on one of the longest building booms in the history of the state penal system.

If present trends continue, the California prison population will rise from 141,000 to more than 200,000 by 2000. Slightly more than 50,000 inmates will be doing time for drug-related offenses.

Assuming today's prices—which do not include the expense of building more prisons—drug-related felons could cost taxpayers $500 million to $1 billion a year to incarcerate by the end of the twentieth century.

"We've taken the tough-on-crime approach to drugs. Now we have to figure out what to do with the increasing numbers of people in prison. Treatment is a good way to go. It's cheap and it works," said Harry K. Wexler, a researcher for the National Development and Research Institute, a New York-based think tank that specializes in criminal justice issues.

> *"Incarceration alone . . . does not necessarily stop addiction or protect the public in the long run."*

For almost two decades, Wexler has studied prison substance abuse programs nationwide. His findings show that the re-incarceration rate for Amity, including dropouts, is about 20% lower than for untreated convicts two years after release from prison. It is estimated that about 65% of untreated convicts are rearrested within the same time period.

The most dramatic reductions occurred among program graduates who received several months of treatment at Amity's outside facility. Of that group, 16% were rearrested.

The California Department of Corrections estimates that if Amity treats 2,100 inmates over seven years at a cost of $1.5 million a year, taxpayers would recoup the program's expenses and save $4.7 million in prison costs due to reduced recidivism.

> *"Authorities expected that 25% of inmates [in Donovan State Prison's drug program] would test positive, but only one did—for marijuana."*

Assuming that Amity-style programs were established in all 32 state prisons, taxpayers' potential savings could be as high as $150 million over seven years if the current level of success were maintained.

And that does not reveal the total savings. Convicts who go straight no longer tax the police, court and social welfare system. The analysis also does not include other benefits to the corrections system, such as less violence and fewer violations of prison rules.

Amity "is doing better than I ever anticipated," said Donovan Warden John Ratelle. "If we had only a 10% reduction in recidivism, that would be a success. It is worth the money to do what we are doing."

He grew even more convinced that the program was making progress when he ordered surprise urine tests at the treatment unit in 1991. The random testing was conducted on a Monday because prison drug use is often heaviest on weekends. Authorities expected that 25% of inmates would test positive, but only one did—for marijuana.

Even the Unwilling Get Drawn into the Process

In many ways, prisons are perfect settings for drug treatment. There is a large captive audience. Inmates are often motivated by many factors from sheer boredom to measures that have increased sentences for repeat offenders, such as California's three-strikes law.

Even the unwilling get drawn into the process despite themselves, such as Rocky R. Reeder, a heroin addict and habitual criminal who applied to Amity just to stop his transfer to a prison in Northern California.

Reeder, 41, of San Diego, had been a one-man crime wave. By his own estimate, he stole more than 70 vehicles, and each week burglarized two or three houses for much of his career. If someone was sleeping on the sofa or taking a shower when he entered, the bigger the thrill.

He went to juvenile hall and the California Youth Authority more than a dozen times. He has been sent to prison seven times, the last to Donovan in 1992 for possession of stolen property.

"At first, I didn't care about treatment," he said. "But I started listening to the leaders in group therapy. They were just like me. It made a difference. The person had been there, and I could relate."

Reeder, who has been off drugs since May 1992, works with his son as a technician for a water purification business. He realizes he can never apologize to his victims, so he occasionally visits Amity's parolee program and counsels those in treatment.

"Many convicts are amenable to changing their behavior," said Lewis Yablonsky, an expert on residential treatment programs and professor emeritus of sociology and criminology at Cal State Northridge. "Amity is a small program even in Donovan, but it is a significant demonstration of what can be done."

He predicts that well-run treatment projects in every state prison could significantly reduce the inmate population.

Expanding Treatment

Substance abuse treatment has been added to two other prisons since Amity arrived at Donovan. The Correctional Institute for Women in Frontera opened the Forever Free program for 120 inmates several years ago. An 80-bed facility called Walden House has begun at the California Rehabilitation Center in Norco.

In late 1997, the first 1,056 beds of a 1,456-bed facility will open at Corcoran. The Corcoran program will more than triple the statewide capacity of treatment for convicts—a crucial test to see if drug rehabilitation can work on a large scale.

> *"Well-run treatment projects in every state prison could significantly reduce the inmate population."*

"I don't think we have seen a serious effort at prison treatment until the last few years," said John Erickson, director of substance abuse programs for the Department of Corrections. "There is now an all-out effort to refine treatment strategies."

He said adding large numbers of treatment beds to the prison system has gone slowly because reliable research has not been available in California until the last few years.

Whether drug treatment will be expanded on a massive scale is hard to predict, even with more positive research. Legislators, government officials and correctional officers worry that a broad expansion might compromise the quality of smaller, successful programs like Amity.

"People need to be convinced that this is more than an aberration," said Rod Mullen, president of the Amity Foundation. "They need to see this as something as normal as a prison industry program, or a religious program or a high school education program. But that kind of shift in attitude does not happen overnight."

Indeed, it hasn't. The first drug and alcohol programs for convicts were established in the 1930s at two federal prisons in Lexington, Ky., and Fort Worth, Texas. Because such efforts were poorly administered and ineffective, criminal justice experts came to believe that little could be done to rehabilitate convicts.

That attitude did not begin to change until the early 1980s, when a substance abuse treatment program called Stay 'N' Out reported some substantial success at the Arthur Kill State Prison on Staten Island, N.Y.

As more positive results emerged from a program in Oregon, the federal government began to fund pilot projects across the country. Since then, encouraging findings have been reported in California, Delaware and Texas.

A Cautious Approach

Still, many public officials approach the issue with caution. Craig L. Brown, California finance director, said many legislators and bureaucrats would be more encouraged about prison drug treatment if the improvements could be demonstrated at five years after release, instead of the two years now used for research purposes.

"There are some people who think drug treatment has marginal impact and is not long-lasting enough," Brown said. "On the other hand the existing projects have been well-researched with good scientific methods. Everything looks very promising, but you can't say it's a slam-dunk winner right now."

Among those who are now believers is [California] state Senate Democratic Leader Bill Lockyer of Hayward. He introduced legislation in March 1997 that would add 4,000 treatment slots to the corrections system by 2002. The proposal has some bipartisan support.

The state legislative analyst's office estimates that the expansion might save taxpayers $36 million a year in addition to a one-time savings of $85 million by avoiding the construction of facilities for 2,000 inmates.

> *"As more positive results emerged from a program in Oregon, the federal government began to fund pilot projects across the country."*

"The current policy of building more prisons wastes money and doesn't rehabilitate those in situations where it might work," Lockyer said. "I don't consider myself a do-gooder or a liberal on the issue. If this can help a convict, improve public safety and save money, that sounds like a winner to me."

Cocaine Treatment Programs Are Effective

by RAND Corporation

About the author: *The RAND Corporation is a public policy research organization with headquarters in Santa Monica, California.*

One doesn't hear much these days about the war on drugs or the cocaine epidemic of the 1980s that provoked it. A major reason the bellicose rhetoric has subsided and drug-related crime stories have migrated to the inside pages of the nation's newspapers is that the number of people using cocaine has dropped sharply—from more than 12 million in the early to mid-1980s to 5 million in 1992. Are we to conclude that the threat, if not over, is at least contained and that society has emerged the winner?

Unfortunately, the answer is no. Despite the large decline in the number of users and the expenditure of tens of billions of dollars on law enforcement, the total amount of cocaine consumed in the United States has been stuck at its mid-1980s peak for almost a decade.

A pathbreaking study by RAND researchers C. Peter Rydell and Susan S. Everingham explains this seeming paradox: The number of heavy users is growing, making up in consumption for the overall decline in the number of users. Further, the analysis shows, the current policy emphasis on stemming the supply of cocaine is far less effective in reducing consumption—and more expensive—than treatment programs aimed at controlling demand.

Seven Times More Effective

Treatment is seven times more cost-effective in reducing cocaine consumption than the best supply-control program and could cut consumption by a third if it were extended to all heavy users, according to the study. Such a strategy could also substantially reduce the number of users and the costs they inflict on society through crime and lost productivity.

The study shows past trends and predicts future trends in cocaine consump-

From RAND Corporation, "Treatment: Effective (but Unpopular) Weapon Against Drugs," *RAND Research Review*, Spring 1995. (This article is based on the following research reports: "Controlling Cocaine: Supply vs. Demand Programs" by C. Peter Rydell and Susan S. Everingham, RAND/MR-331-ONDCP/A/DPRC, 1994, and "Modeling the Demand for Cocaine" by Susan S. Everingham and C. Peter Rydell, RAND/MR-332-ONDCP/A/DPRC, 1994.) Reprinted by permission of RAND Corporation.

tion. It demonstrates how the shares of consumption attributable to light and heavy users have been changing and what these patterns seem to imply for cocaine-control policy. Finally, and most strikingly, it provides the first systematic method of comparing the cost-effectiveness of cocaine-control programs.

The researchers estimate there are now about two million heavy cocaine users—and they consume substantially more cocaine per capita than do light users. Heavy (once a week or more) users account for over two-thirds of today's cocaine demand, up from less than one-half in 1980. Clearly, consumption will remain high unless these heavy users reduce their consumption or quit altogether.

Evaluating control programs requires comparing their effects as well as their costs. But supply-control programs and demand-control programs produce different kinds of results. The researchers compare them by identifying a common measure—the annual program cost required to reduce U.S. consumption of cocaine by a given amount: The lower that cost, the more cost-effective the program.

Treatment for heavy users is more cost-effective in reducing cocaine consumption than domestic enforcement, the most efficient of the three supply-control programs studied. For example, cocaine consumption can be reduced over 15 years by an average of 1 percent per year by spending an additional $34 million per year for treatment. To achieve the same effect, we would have to spend annually an additional $250 million for law enforcement efforts against drug dealers and their agents, or $370 million for interdicting the drug at our borders, or $780 million to help foreign governments cut supplies at the source.

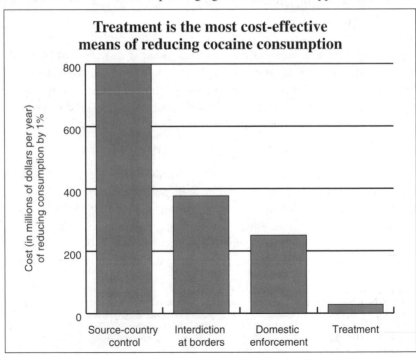

Treatment is the most cost-effective means of reducing cocaine consumption

Supply control becomes more cost-effective as drugs move away from the source through the pipeline toward the consumer. Thus, interdiction at the border is less than one-half as costly as source-country control, domestic enforcement only two-thirds as costly as interdiction at the border. But treatment is the winner by a wide margin because it is less costly relative to its effects.

> *"Treatment is seven times more cost-effective in reducing cocaine consumption than the best supply-control program."*

"These results suggest that if one were going to spend an additional dollar on drug control, it should be spent on treatment, not on a supply-control program," the authors declare. Or if the choice is to make cocaine-control policies more cost-effective within current spending levels, "cut back on supply control and expand treatment of heavy users." They emphasize, however, that treatment is not in itself a solution and that deep cuts in enforcement funding would be counterproductive.

An Unpopular Approach

Despite the advantages of demand-control programs, Congress has been loath to fund them. They are unpopular with middle-class taxpayers, too, who see drug treatment as wasting money on a group of people who can't be trusted and who have no desire to be helped.

"There is understandable skepticism about spending taxpayer dollars on these programs when only a small fraction of drug users who get treatment manage to quit for good," acknowledges Jonathan Caulkins, codirector of RAND's drug policy research center, within which the study was conducted. "But that is looking at the problem from the wrong end of the telescope. The programs work and should be funded—not because they are the cure for drug addiction, but because they effectively cut consumption and consumption is what drives the drug trade."

The United States at all levels, public and private, currently spends an estimated $13 billion on these four types of cocaine-control programs, only $1 billion of which goes for treatment. The study explores several alternative spending mixes that promise to improve on current policy.

One option—boosting the cocaine treatment budget to $4 billion by reallocating 25 percent of supply-control spending—would provide enough dollars to treat all heavy users once each year (versus the 30 percent treated today). The effects, according to the analysis, would include a one-third reduction in annual cocaine consumption, a significant drop in the number of users and, as a result, a decrease in the cocaine-related costs of crime and lost productivity, which have been estimated by others as $10 billion annually.

Expanding treatment so much, even with adequate funding, would be difficult because some heavy users may refuse treatment or prove difficult to find. Enforcement is important in this regard because it is one means of inducing users to accept treatment. Expanding treatment beyond $4 billion annually, however, is probably infeasible because of diminishing returns.

Demand Control Cuts Use Directly

Supply-control programs discourage drug consumption indirectly by raising the street price. Drug seizures, asset seizures, arrests and imprisonment increase the costs of producing and distributing the drug, and these costs are passed along to retail buyers.

Treatment cuts consumption directly, rather than through the price mechanism, and in two stages—during and after treatment. The study uses conservative estimates, derived from the literature, of the effects of treatment: Previous studies have shown that 80 percent of people in treatment stay off drugs while there, a consumption-reducing effect that is often overlooked; in addition, an estimated 13 percent of heavy users stop or reduce heavy use, some permanently and others at least for awhile, as a result of treatment.

"Cocaine treatment also has an advantage over supply-control programs in terms of consumption of other drugs," Rydell comments. "Raising the price of cocaine may increase consumption of other drugs by inducing cocaine users to switch. Treatment might reduce such consumption since many cocaine users use other drugs as well."

> *"Results suggest that if one were going to spend an additional dollar on drug control, it should be spent on treatment."*

The study's conclusions are based on many assumptions, the authors point out, in particular the responsiveness of consumption to price increases and of heavy users to treatment. Even over a very wide range of reasonable assumptions, however, the cost advantages of treatment over supply control and of one supply-control program over another are so great that their ranking is not in doubt.

Methadone Is an Effective Treatment for Heroin Addiction

by Jennifer McNeely

About the author: *Jennifer McNeely is a former senior research associate for the Lindesmith Center, a New York City policy research institute that focuses on drug policy and related issues. She is now a consultant to the center.*

Methadone, a long-acting synthetic narcotic analgesic, was first used in the maintenance treatment of drug addiction in the mid-1960s, by Drs. Vincent Dole and Marie Nyswander of Rockefeller University. There are now 115,000 methadone maintenance patients in the U.S. Forty thousand of them are in New York State, and about half that many are in California. Methadone is widely employed throughout the world, and is the most effective known treatment for heroin addiction.

The Goal of Treatment

The goal of methadone maintenance treatment (MMT) is to reduce illegal heroin use and the crime, death, disease, and other negative consequences associated with addiction. Methadone can be used to detoxify heroin addicts, but most heroin addicts who detox—using methadone or any other method—return to heroin use. Therefore, the goal of methadone maintenance treatment is to reduce and even eliminate heroin use among addicts by stabilizing them on methadone for as long as is necessary to help them keep their lives together and avoid returning to previous patterns of drug use. The benefits of methadone maintenance treatment have been established by hundreds of scientific studies, and there are almost no negative health consequences of long-term methadone treatment, even when it continues for twenty or thirty years.

The success of methadone in reducing crime, death, disease, and drug use is well documented.

Methadone is the most effective treatment for heroin addiction.

Compared to the other major drug treatment modalities—drug-free outpatient treatment, therapeutic communities, and chemical dependency treatment—methadone is the most rigorously studied and has yielded the best results.

Methadone is effective HIV/AIDS prevention.

MMT reduces the frequency of injecting and of needle sharing. Methadone treatment is also an important point of contact with service providers, and supplies an opportunity to teach drug users harm reduction techniques such as how to prevent HIV/AIDS, hepatitis, and other health problems—including abscesses, dermatitis, and overdoses—that endanger drug users.

Methadone treatment reduces criminal behavior.

Drug offense arrests decline because MMT patients reduce or stop buying and using illegal drugs. Arrests for predatory crimes decline because MMT patients no longer need to finance a costly heroin addiction, and because treatment allows many patients to stabilize their lives and return to legitimate employment.

Methadone drastically reduces, and often eliminates, heroin use among addicts.

> *"MMT . . . reduces the criminal behavior associated with illegal drug use, promotes health, and improves social productivity."*

The Treatment Outcome Prospective Study (TOPS)—the largest contemporary controlled study of drug treatment—found that patients drastically reduced their heroin use while in treatment, with less than 10% using heroin weekly or daily after just three months in treatment. After two years or more, heroin use among MMT patients declines, on average, to 15% of pre-treatment levels. Often, use of other drugs—including cocaine, sedatives, and even alcohol—also declines when an opiate addict enters methadone treatment, even though methadone has no direct pharmacological effect on non-opiate drug craving.

Methadone is cost effective.

MMT, which costs on average about $4,000 per patient per year, reduces the criminal behavior associated with illegal drug use, promotes health, and improves social productivity, all of which serve to reduce the societal costs of drug addiction. Incarceration, by comparison, costs $20,000 to $40,000 per year. Residential drug treatment programs cost $13–20,000/year. Furthermore, given that only 5–10% of the cost of MMT actually pays for the medication itself, methadone could be prescribed and delivered even less expensively, through physicians in general medical practice, low-service clinics, and pharmacies.

Alternate Means

Methadone is effective outside of traditional clinic settings. Methadone in the U.S. is generally restricted to specialized methadone clinics, which are subject to a host of counseling and other service requirements mandated by federal, state, and municipal regulators. Though limited, experiments with providing methadone through alternate means have had positive results.

Limited Service Methadone Maintenance. Limited service MMT is a low-cost method of providing methadone treatment services to addicts who cannot or will not access comprehensive methadone programs. Though limited service programs may not be as effective as the best

> *"[MMT patients] do not seek out the drug in the absence of withdrawal symptoms or pain, and their lives do not revolve around drug use."*

full service programs, their patients do substantially reduce drug use and typically fare better than do illicit drug users not enrolled in any programs.

Physician Prescribing. MMT as part of general medical practice is common throughout Europe, Australia, and New Zealand, but is severely restricted in the U.S. There have been U.S. "medical maintenance" trials, which permitted some long-term methadone recipients to transfer from traditional methadone clinics to hospital-based physicians. Medical maintenance, where tested, has achieved excellent treatment results. Medical maintenance is also cost effective, and patients prefer it over traditional methadone clinics.

Questions About Methadone

How does methadone work?

Methadone is an opiate agonist which has a series of actions similar to those of morphine and other narcotic medications. Heroin addicts are physically dependent on opiate drugs, and will experience withdrawal symptoms if the concentration of opiates in the body falls below a certain level. In maintenance treatment, patients are given enough methadone to ward off opiate withdrawal symptoms, but not enough to induce narcotic effects.

Does methadone make patients "high" or interfere with normal functioning?

No. Used in maintenance treatment, in proper doses, methadone does not create euphoria, sedation, or analgesia. Methadone has no adverse effects on motor skills, mental capability, or employability.

What is the proper dose of methadone?

Dose must be individually determined, because of differences in metabolism, body weight, and opiate tolerance. The proper maintenance dose is one at which narcotic craving is averted—without creating euphoria, sedation, or analgesia—for 24–36 hours. Doses of 60–100 mg, and sometimes more, are required for most patients, and doses below 60 mg are almost always insufficient for patients who wish to abstain from heroin use.

Is methadone more addictive than heroin?

Physical dependence and tolerance to a drug are part of addiction, but they're not the whole story. Addiction is characterized by compulsive use of the drug despite adverse consequences. The MMT patient is no more an addict than the terminal cancer patient who is physically dependent on morphine, or the diabetic who is dependent on insulin. They do not seek out the drug in the absence of withdrawal symptoms or pain, and their lives do not revolve around drug use.

Is methadone harder to kick than heroin?

Symptoms of abrupt withdrawal are qualitatively similar when the amount of drug used is pharmacologically equivalent, but withdrawal from heroin tends to be intense and fairly brief, while methadone withdrawal is less acute and longer lasting. Withdrawal symptoms can be ameliorated by tapering the dose over an extended period of time.

Length of Treatment

Is methadone maintenance treatment for life?

Some patients remain in methadone treatment for more than ten years, and even for the rest of their lives, but they constitute a minority (5–20%) of patients.

How long should treatment last?

Generally, the length of time spent in treatment is positively related to treatment success. The duration of treatment should be individually and clinically determined, and treatment should last for as long as the physician and the individual patient agree is appropriate. Federal, and often state, regulations require annual evaluation of patients to determine whether they should continue in MMT.

Is methadone a desirable street drug, with high potential for abuse?

Though methadone is sometimes sold on the illicit drug market, most buyers of diverted methadone are active heroin users who won't or can't get into a methadone program. The extent of abuse associated with diverted methadone is small relative to heroin and cocaine, and primary addiction to methadone is rare. While methadone, like almost any drug, can cause overdoses if used improperly, overdose deaths attributed to methadone alone are few, and are incidental compared to heroin deaths. The Drug Abuse Warning Network found, in its 1994 sample of emergency room incidents, 15 methadone deaths, 251 heroin/morphine deaths, and 13 aspirin deaths. Finally, not all methadone overdose deaths are necessarily caused by illicitly purchased methadone; some are undoubtedly the result of accidental or inappropriate consumption of legally obtained methadone.

> *"Concerns about methadone's effects on the immune system and on the kidneys, liver, and heart have been laid to rest."*

Does methadone interfere with good health?

Scientific studies have shown that the most significant health consequence of long term methadone treatment is a marked improvement in general health. Concerns about methadone's effects on the immune system and on the kidneys, liver, and heart have been laid to rest. Methadone's most common side effects—constipation and sweating—usually fade with time, and are not serious health hazards.

Is it safe to take methadone during pregnancy?

MMT during pregnancy does not impair the child's developmental and cognitive functioning, and it is the medically recommended course of treatment for most pregnant opiate-dependent women.

Is methadone maintenance appropriate for all drug users?

No. Methadone is a treatment for opiate dependence, and is not appropriate for individuals who use heroin but are not, and have not been, dependent. There are also drug-free treatment options and, increasingly, other medications—including buprenorphine and LAAM [long-acting methadone]—that may be appropriate for some users.

The D.A.R.E. Program Has Been Ineffective

by James Bovard

About the author: *James Bovard is the author of* Shakedown: How Government Screws You from A to Z.

American schools are providing more anti-drug use education than ever before, primarily through the DARE program—Drug Abuse Resistance Education. Federal, state, and local governments and private donors are spending roughly $700 million a year on DARE, which is currently being taught by police officers to more than 5 million children in more than 250,000 classrooms each year.

DARE Everywhere

DARE in operation sometimes resembles a religious crusade. As an article in the *Minneapolis Star Tribune* noted, "Schools in Minnesota fly the DARE flag. Students can buy DARE frisbees, wear a DARE wristwatch or sing the official DARE song." Students are also able to win or purchase DARE pencils, erasers, workbooks, and certificates of achievement. There are DARE bears, DARE jeeps driven by police, and DARE bumper stickers as far as the eye can see. Politicians love it, of course, and none more so than Bill Clinton. During his State of the Union address on January 23, 1996, the president pointed to his special guests seated in the balcony and declared, "People like these DARE officers are making a real impression on grade school children that will give them the strength to say no when the time comes."

The DARE curriculum is taught by police primarily to fifth and sixth graders one hour a week for seventeen weeks, though children as young as kindergarten and as old as senior high school also receive DARE instruction. The police serve as role models, trusted confidants, and wise men and women. Unfortunately, DARE appears to be relatively ineffective at preventing drug abuse, and is far less effective than some competing drug education programs.

The federal Bureau of Justice Assistance, the research branch of the U.S. Justice Department, paid $300,000 to the Research Triangle Institute (RTI), a North Carolina research firm, to conduct an analysis of the effectiveness of DARE. RTI researchers completed their report and submitted it to the Justice Department in February 1994—whereupon the Justice Department refused to publish it, the first report out of hundreds commissioned in recent years that the agency refused to print. A summary of the report was finally published by the *American Journal of Public Health* in September 1994.

> *"DARE was found to be less effective [than other methods] in every category— knowledge and attitudes towards drugs, social skills, and drug use itself."*

The RTI study found that DARE has been far less effective at discouraging drug abuse than have other "interactive" teaching methods. DARE was found to be less effective in every category—knowledge and attitudes towards drugs, social skills, and drug use itself. RTI concluded:

> For drug use, the average effect size for interactive programs was three times greater than the average DARE effect size; for social skills, four times greater than DARE; and for attitudes, three times greater. These findings suggest that greater effectiveness is possible with school-based drug use prevention programs for fifth- and sixth-grade pupils than is achieved by the original DARE core curriculum.

Overall, DARE was found to deter drug, alcohol, or tobacco use in only a statistically insignificant three percent of program participants. DARE's minimal deterrence was achieved via discouraging the use of alcohol and tobacco, not illicit drugs. Researchers concluded that "DARE's limited influence on adolescent drug behavior contrasts with the program's popularity and prevalence. An important implication is that DARE could be taking the place of other, more beneficial drug-use curricula."

Getting Tips from Children

DARE's use of police officers as instructors has also come under attack. As a report by a committee of concerned Massachusetts parents from the Ashfield-Sanfield school district concluded in June 1995, "There is nothing new about police coming into schools to teach survival skills. What is new about DARE is police coming into schools to teach attitudes and mental health." Unfortunately, some police have had other things in mind. In the official DARE Implementation Guide, police are advised to be alert for signs of children who have relatives who use drugs. As officers of the law, these DARE instructors are duty bound to follow up leads that might come to their attention through inadvertent or indiscreet comments by young children.

After police win the children's trust, children sometimes confide to the police the names of people the children suspect are illegally using drugs. For example, nine-year-old Darrin Davis of Douglasville, Georgia, called 911 after he found a small amount of speed hidden in his parents' bedroom, because, as he told a reporter:

> At school, they told us that if we ever see drugs, call 911 because people who use drugs need help. . . . I thought the police would come get the drugs and tell them that drugs are wrong. They never said they would arrest them. It didn't say that in the video. The police officer held me by the shoulder and made me watch them put handcuffs on my mom and dad and put them in the police car. I always thought police were honest and told the truth. But in court, I heard them tell the judge that I wanted my mom and dad arrested. That is a lie. I did not tell them that.

Both parents lost their jobs, a bank threatened to foreclose on their home, and his father was kept in jail for three months. Darrin became so agitated that he burnt down part of a neighbor's house because he said he wanted to be with his father in jail. Darrin's parents later filed for a divorce; according to Jay Bouldin, the Davises' attorney, the strain caused by the bust played a major role in destroying their marriage.

DARE spokeswoman Roberta Silverman argued that drug busts which occur after the training are often unfairly linked to DARE. But the *Wall Street Journal* noted in 1992: "In two recent cases in Boston, children who had tipped police stepped out of their homes carrying DARE diplomas as police arrived to arrest their parents." Similar DARE-related drug busts of parents have been reported in Colorado, Oklahoma, Maryland, and Maine.

> *"In Boston, children who had tipped police stepped out of their homes carrying DARE diplomas as police arrived to arrest their parents."*

DARE officials stress that the program does not encourage children to turn in family members for violating laws against drug use. But if that is not the program's intention, surely it is a result of its propaganda materials. One of the DARE lessons that police give students in kindergarten through fourth grade emphasizes DARE's "Three R's": "Recognize, Resist, and Report." The official DARE Officer's Guide for Grades K–4 contains a worksheet that instructs children to "Circle the names of the people you could tell if . . . a friend finds some pills"; the "Police" are listed along with "Mother or Father," "Teacher," or "Friend." The next exercise instructs children to check off whom they should inform if "asked to keep a secret"—"Police" is again listed as an option. The idea that anyone should keep a secret from the proper authorities is apparently intolerable.

Drug Treatment Programs Are Often Ineffective

by William J. Bennett and John P. Walters

About the authors: *William J. Bennett is a codirector of Empower America, a conservative public policy research organization in Washington, D.C. John P. Walters is the president of the Philanthropic Roundtable, a Washington, D.C., organization of grantmakers and corporate foundations.*

Today's addicts are the most visible casualties of the permissive culture and the drug fad of the late 1960s, the 1970s and the early 1980s. These addicts have moved up in the ranks from casual users. They are largely aging, never married and predominantly male. Most commit crimes—including selling drugs—as a means of income to purchase drugs. They also are concentrated largely among blacks and live in our inner cities. While these addicts constitute the single-largest demand for heroin and cocaine in the United States, they also use a variety of other drugs (particularly marijuana) and alcohol.

A Call for More Treatment

The overwhelming reaction to this problem has been a call for more drug treatment. "Treatment on demand" is the preferred weapon of many in the drug fight. In fact, many liberals have argued the rational and humane response to drug addiction is to shift resources from drug enforcement and supply reduction to drug treatment. There are a number of very sophisticated and very effective drug-treatment programs, including very modest ones sponsored by churches using variants of the 12-step method. But the typical discussion of drug treatment in the press and by the government reflects a dangerous ignorance of the most basic facts.

First, the government treatment bureaucracy is manifestly wasteful and ineffective. From fiscal 1988 to fiscal 1994, federal drug-treatment spending almost tripled. At the same time, however, the number of treatment slots remained virtually unchanged and the estimated number of people treated actually declined by 145,000.

Why? As with much of government, it was because the bureaucracies consumed more and more of the resources, leaving less and less for services. Bureaucratic waste and inefficiency aside, the number of addicts served per year, measured in terms of persons served per year, is equivalent to more than half the total estimated number of cocaine and heroin addicts. Clearly, when given the chance, the bulk of these programs are not that successful.

In addition, federal treatment funds continue to be distributed largely on the basis of population, even though we know that addicts are concentrated in our major cities. And there has been no effort to ensure that addicts are placed in appropriate programs. Today, outpatient treatment slots predominate when most experts argue that the only reasonable hope of successfully treating today's hard-core addicts is to place them in long-term, residential treatment. Bush administration efforts to make programs accountable—to cut off support to those that did not produce results and match resources with the need—were not enacted by the Democratic leadership in Congress. And the Clinton administration has abandoned all such efforts.

Drug Courts

In the 1994 crime bill, large sums were offered for drug courts. These provisions were highlighted by liberals who announced that they were being "smart and tough." The model, and essentially the justification, for this funding was Miami's drug court and Attorney General Janet Reno's personal involvement with it as a prosecutor. But in August 1994, as the fight about the crime bill was near its peak, the *Miami Herald* published a lengthy report raising serious questions about the effectiveness of the program. In particular, the program established to divert first- and second-time drug offenders into treatment instead of prison was being used by robbers and burglars to serve as little as 45 days. And in December 1994, the *Herald* reported that the chief judge overseeing the Miami drug court ordered an audit of the entire program, expressing alarm that it "had no mechanism to measure whether it was succeeding."

> *"The government treatment bureaucracy is manifestly wasteful and ineffective."*

A central flaw in the rush to embrace drug courts as a major answer to addiction and crime is that a very large number of addicted offenders today are long-term, hard-core addicts who are poorly suited for a diversion program. Drug courts, properly run, may hold promise for treating young addicts. But young addicts are not the primary problem.

In reviewing all forms of cocaine treatment, a study by the White House drug office, conducted by the Rand Corp., found that 20 percent of addicts continue using drugs while in treatment and only 13.2 percent of the cocaine addicts treated reduce their drug use below weekly or more frequent use (what Rand defined as "heavy use") during the year following their treatment. Overall,

Rand reported, cocaine treatment is only 4 percent effective in reducing heavy use and only 2 percent more effective in reducing heavy use than no treatment at all.

The Harsh Reality

While we should continue to support treatment programs, we need to face the harsh reality of cocaine and crack addiction: Most addicts are likely to die from the effects of their addiction sometime in their 40s, if not earlier. This is yet one more compelling reason why preventing casual drug use by young people—the first step on the path to addiction—is so important.

As long as the drug problem is discussed in terms of treatment vs. enforcement or supply vs. demand, it will remain fundamentally misguided. These dogmatic positions are at odds with both reality and common sense. An effective drug policy should begin with this assumption: As long as young people and those who receive treatment reside in communities in which the supply of dangerous, addictive drugs remains plentiful—that is, where there is de facto legalization—prevention and, especially, treatment efforts will be severely undercut and for purposes of national policy, ineffective.

"Overall, Rand reported, cocaine treatment is only 4 percent effective in reducing heavy use and only 2 percent more effective in reducing heavy use than no treatment at all."

Classroom Drug Education Has Been a Failure

by Phyllis Schlafly

About the author: Phyllis Schlafly is the founder of the political action group Eagle Forum and the publisher of the monthly Phyllis Schlafly Report.

The alarming rise in illegal drug use by teenagers is big news. Although drug use by adults has leveled off and is actually down since 1985, drug use (mostly in marijuana) among teens aged 12 to 17 is increasing every year, doubling since 1992 to eleven percent in 1995.

Marijuana damages the memory, energy and general learning power of children. Children who start out on marijuana are 17 times more likely to progress to hard drugs than if they had never used marijuana.

A Scary Drug Problem

The drug experts call this "very scary." Their explanations include neglect by parents, the misleading messages from political leaders, the glamorization of drugs by the entertainment industry, the failure of the media to cover the issue, and denial of the problem.

There is another reason they are overlooking: the failure of drug education in the schools. So-called drug education may even be counterproductive. On a youth roundtable on drugs on the *Lehrer NewsHour* on September 25, 1996, one teen offered his explanation that drug courses in school actually *cause* experimentation with illegal drugs.

Congress has poured billions (not just millions) of taxpayers' dollars into drug education in public schools. In 1991, Congress's watchdog agency, the General Accounting Office (GAO) reported to the Senate on the $1.1 billion that had been spent on drug education up to that date. The cover of the report summed up the result: "Impact Unknown."

The GAO report listed 21 classroom drug curricula commonly used in public schools. They typically presented students with a lot of "nonjudgmental information" combined with a process of "decision making" that urged students to

From Phyllis Schlafly, "Why Are More Kids Doing Drugs?" *Phyllis Schlafly Report*, October 1996. Reprinted with permission.

consider the "alternatives." A couple of courses vaguely described "refusal skills," but not a single course was based on a "just say no" approach, or stated that illegal drugs are wrong, or warned students that they must not consider the "alternative" of using illegal drugs. The courses did not comply with the Drug-Free Schools and Communities Act which requires all public schools to teach that "the use of illicit drugs and the unlawful possession and use of alcohol is wrong."

Teaching students that anything is "wrong" is so anathema to public school curriculum writers that they simply ignore the law's mandate. Under prevailing public school methodology, all teaching (especially about sex and drugs) is "non-directive." For example, the GAO report described a drug education course called "Me-ology." It called for sixth grade students to spend 17 hours of class time "choosing actions that conform to personal beliefs after considering alternative choices." The course did not teach that it would be wrong to choose cocaine as the "alternative" that conforms to their personal beliefs.

The GAO descriptions of the 21 drug curricula show that most of the courses spend most of their class time playing psychological games under the rubric of "enhancing students' self-awareness and self-esteem." The education theorists have convinced themselves that drug abuse is caused by students' lack of self-esteem.

DARE: No Lasting Effects

Subsequent investigations of drug education courses have produced similar disappointing results. Dr. Richard Clayton, director of the Center for Prevention Research at the University of Kentucky in Lexington, told the *New York Times* on September 18, 1996, that the popular course called DARE (Drug Abuse Resistance Education) "has been evaluated in a reasonably rigorous way by five to ten different researchers in different parts of the country," but researchers "failed to find lasting effects."

In 1995, the Michigan State Senate exposed a giant scandal in the use of federal anti-drug funds by the Michigan State Department of Education. The bureaucrats had illegally diverted more than $50 million of federal anti-drug funds into pressuring local school districts to adopt the bureaucrats' pet project: a controversial health, sex and psychological curriculum called the "Michigan Model."

Some diverted funds were spent on an organized campaign to discredit

> *"Not a single course was based on a 'just say no' approach, or stated that illegal drugs are wrong."*

and intimidate parents by keeping files on parents, making photos and videos of them, training coordinators how to "handle" parents, having a computer bulletin board to exchange information on parents, labeling them with epithets, and inviting People for the American Way to assist in the anti-parent campaign.

Meanwhile, Michigan Drug Control Director, Robert Peterson, was reporting alarmingly high drug-use rates among Michigan youth. Maybe the teenagers wouldn't have fared any better if the money had been spent on non-directive drug education (instead of sex and psychology), but the illegal diversion of funds shows that the educators just weren't interested in addressing the increased use of drugs by teenagers, even when they were given plenty of funds to deal with the problem.

> *"The scandal of what is called drug education is ripe for a thorough Congressional investigation."*

According to the GAO report cited above, federal drug education funds were also diverted to psychological and attitudinal "touchy-feely" courses in Los Angeles and Cleveland. Nancy Reagan's "just say no" campaign never made it into the classroom.

The scandal of what is called drug education is ripe for a thorough Congressional investigation. Exposing the misuse of the funds already spent will not only help us to tackle increased drug use by teenagers, but it will go a long way toward showing parents that the public schools have taught children it's okay to make their own behavioral choices without regard to standards of right and wrong.

Chapter 4

Should Illegal Drugs Be Legalized?

Chapter Preface

On the cover of its February 12, 1996, issue, the conservative *National Review* proclaimed, "THE WAR ON DRUGS IS LOST." According to the magazine's editors, including well-known commentator William F. Buckley Jr.,

> It is our judgment that the war on drugs has failed, . . . it is wasting our resources, and it is encouraging civil, judicial and penal procedures associated with police states. We all agree on movement toward legalization.

Buckley and other proponents of legalizing drugs argue that in order to relieve crowded courts and prisons and to eradicate the crime and violence associated with the illegal drug trade, America has no choice but to make drugs legally available. According to the Libertarian Party, half of the nation's spending on law enforcement and prisons goes toward fighting drug-related crime. The party maintains that legalization would wipe out drug traffickers and would result in lower prices for drugs, allowing drug users to "support their habits with honest work, rather than by crime."

On the other hand, opponents contend that legalizing drugs would increase, not reduce, rates of crime and violence. These observers maintain that legalization would produce millions of additional drug users, many of whom would commit crime or violence while under the influence of dangerous drugs. Former National Institute of Drug Abuse director Robert DuPont estimates that legalization could raise the number of users of cocaine and marijuana by as many as sixty million. According to Columbia University's Center on Addiction and Substance Abuse, "Legalization would increase the number of hard-core addicts, increase drug-related problems and costs, and increase crime."

The legalization of drugs would amount to a drastic change in America's drug policy, involving many complexities and uncertainties. The authors in the following chapter debate whether drug legalization would help or harm drug users and society at large.

Illegal Drugs Should Be Legalized

by Walter Wink

About the author: *Walter Wink is a biblical professor at Auburn Theological Seminary in New York City.*

The Quaker commitment to nonviolence has direct implications for the United States' failed drug war. It is a spiritual law that we become what we hate. Jesus articulated this law in the Sermon on the Mount when he admonished, "Do not react violently to the one who is evil" (Scholars' Version). The sense is clear: do not resist evil by violent means; do not let evil set the terms of your response. Applied to the drug issue, this means, "Do not resist drugs by violent methods."

When we oppose evil with the same weapons that evil employs, we commit the same atrocities, violate the same civil liberties, and break the same laws as those whom we oppose. We become what we hate. Evil makes us over into its double. If one side prevails, the evil continues by virtue of having been established through the means used. This principle of mimetic opposition is abundantly illustrated in the case of the disastrous U.S. drug war.

A Lost War

The drug war is over, and we lost. We merely repeated the mistake of Prohibition. The harder we tried to stamp out this evil, the more lucrative we made it, and the more it spread. Our forcible resistance to evil simply augments it. An evil cannot be eradicated by making it more profitable.

We lost that war on all three fronts: destroying the drug sources, intercepting drugs at our borders, and arresting drug dealers and users.

In the first place, we have failed to cut off drug sources. When we paid Turkey to stop the growth of opium, production merely shifted to Southeast Asia and Afghanistan. Crop substitution programs in Peru led to *increased* planting of coca, as farmers simply planted a small parcel of land with one of the accepted substitute crops and used the bulk of the funds to plant more coca.

From Walter Wink, "Getting Off Drugs: The Legalization Option," *Friends Journal*, February 1996. Reprinted by permission of the author and the *Friends Journal*.

Cocaine cultivation uses only 700 of the 2.5 million square miles suitable for its growth in South America. There is simply no way the United States can police so vast an area.

Second, the drug war has failed to stop illicit drugs at our borders. According to a Government Accounting Office study, the air force spent $3.3 million on drug interdiction, using sophisticated AWACS surveillance planes, over a 15-month period ending in 1987. The grand total of drug seizures from that effort was eight. During the same pe-

> **"The drug war is over, and we lost."**

riod, the combined efforts of the coast guard and navy, sailing for 2,512 ship days at a cost of $40 million, resulted in the seizure of a mere 20 drug-carrying vessels. Hard drugs are so easy to smuggle because they are so concentrated. Our entire country's current annual import of cocaine would fit into a single C-5A cargo plane.

Drug Production and Offenders

As if the flood of imported drugs were not enough, domestic production of marijuana continues to increase. It is the largest cash crop in ten states, and the second largest cash crop in the nation, next only to corn. Methamphetamine, at two to three times the cost of crack, sustains a high for 24 hours as opposed to crack's 20 minutes. It can be manufactured in clandestine laboratories anywhere for an initial cost of only $2,000. Even if we sealed our borders we could not stop the making of new drugs.

Third, the drug war calls for arresting drug dealers and users in the United States. There are already 750,000 drug arrests per year, and the current prison population has far outstripped existing facilities. Drug offenders account for more than 60 percent of the prison population; to make room for them, far more dangerous criminals are being returned to the streets. It is not drugs but the drug laws themselves that have created this monster. The unimaginable wealth involved leads to the corruption of police, judges, and elected officials. A huge bureaucracy has grown dependent on the drug war for employment. Even the financial community is compromised, since the only thing preventing default by some of the heavily indebted Latin American nations or major money-laundering banks is the drug trade. Cocaine brings Bolivia's economy about $600 million per year, a figure equal to the country's total legal export income. Revenues from drug trafficking in Miami, Fla., are greater than those from tourism, exports, health care, and all other legitimate businesses combined.

Murders and Other Casualties

Drug laws have also fostered drug-related murders and an estimated 40 percent of all property crime in the United States. The greatest beneficiaries of the drug laws are drug traffickers, who benefit from the inflated prices that the drug war creates. Rather than collecting taxes on the sale of drugs, governments at all levels expend billions in what amounts to a subsidy of organized criminals. Such are the ironies of violent resistance to evil.

The war on drugs creates other casualties beyond those arrested. There are the ones killed in fights over turf; innocents caught in crossfire; citizens terrified of city streets; escalating robberies; children given free crack to get them addicted and then enlisted as runners and dealers; mothers so crazed for a fix that they abandon their babies, prostitute themselves and their daughters, and addict their unborn. Much of that, too, is the result of the drug laws. Dealing is so lucrative only because it is illegal.

The media usually portray cocaine and crack use as a black ghetto phenomenon. This is a racist caricature. There are more drug addicts among middle- and upper-class whites than any other segment of the population, and far more such occasional drug users. The typical customer is a single, white male 20–40 years old. Only 13 percent of those using illegal drugs are African American, but they constitute 35 percent of those arrested for simple possession and a staggering 74 percent of those sentenced for drug possession. It is the demand by white users that makes drugs flow. Americans consume 60 percent of the world's illegal drugs. That is simply too profitable a market to refuse.

> *"The greatest beneficiaries of the drug laws are drug traffickers, who benefit from the inflated prices that the drug war creates."*

Increasing the budget for fighting drugs is scarcely the answer. As Francis Hall, former head of the New York City Police Department's narcotics division, put it, "It's like [General William C.] Westmoreland asking Washington for two more divisions. We lost the Vietnam War with a half-million men. We're doing the same thing with drugs." The drug war is the United States' longest war, our domestic Vietnam.

We Are the Addicts

This nation is addicted to the use of force, and its armed resistance to the drug trade is doomed to fail precisely because the drug trade perfectly mirrors our own values. We condemn drug traffickers for sacrificing their children, their integrity, and their human dignity just to make money or experience pleasure—without recognizing that these are the values espoused by the society at large. In the drug war, we are scapegoating addicts and blacks for what we have become as a nation. Drugs are the ultimate consumer product for people who want to feel good now without benefit of hard work, social interaction, or making a productive contribution to society. Drug dealers are living out the rags-to-riches American dream as private entrepreneurs desperately trying to become upwardly mobile. That is why we could not win the war on drugs. We are the enemy, and we cannot face that fact. So we launched a half-hearted, half-baked war against a menace that only mirrors ourselves.

The uproar about drugs is itself odd. Illicit drugs are, on the whole, far less dangerous than the legal drugs that many more people consume.

Alcohol is associated with 40 percent of all suicide attempts, 40 percent of all traffic deaths, 54 percent of all violent crimes, and 10 percent of all work-related injuries. Nicotine, the most addictive drug of all, has transformed lung cancer from a medical curiosity to a common disease that now accounts for 3 million deaths a year worldwide, 60 million since the 1950s. Smoking will kill one in three smokers eventually.

> *"Illicit drugs are, on the whole, far less dangerous than the legal drugs that many more people consume."*

None of the illegal drugs is as lethal as tobacco or alcohol. If anyone has ever died as a direct result of marijuana, no one seems to be able to document it. Most deaths from hard drugs are the result of adulteration or unregulated concentrations. Many people can be addicted to heroin for most of their lives without serious health consequences. It has no known side effects other than constipation. Cocaine in powder form is not as addictive as nicotine; only 3 percent of those who try it become addicted. Most cocaine users do not become dependent, and most who do eventually free themselves. Crack is terribly addictive, but its use is a direct consequence of the expense of powdered cocaine, and its spread is in part a function of its lower price.

We must be honest about these facts, because much of the hysteria about illegal drugs has been based on misinformation. All addiction is a serious matter, and Quakers are right to be most concerned about the human costs. But many of these costs are a consequence of a wrongheaded approach to eradication. Our tolerance of the real killer-drugs (nicotine and alcohol) and our abhorrence of the drugs that are far less lethal is hypocritical, or at best a selective moralism reflecting passing fashions of indignation.

Drug addiction is singled out as evil, yet ours is a society of addicts. We project on the black drug subculture all our profound anxieties about our own addictions (to wealth, power, sex, food, work, religion, alcohol, caffeine, and tobacco) and attack addiction in others without having to gain insight about ourselves. New York City councilman Wendell Foster illustrated this scapegoating attitude when he suggested chaining addicts to trees so people could spit on them. Instead of nurturing compassion in order to help addicts, our society targets them as pariahs and dumps on them our own shadow side.

A Better Strategy

I'm not advocating giving up the war on drugs because we can't win. I'm saying that we lost because we let drugs dictate the means we used to oppose them. We have to break out of the spiral of mimetic violence. The only way to do so is to ruin the world market price of drugs by legalizing them. We have to repeal this failed Second Prohibition. The moment the price of drugs plummets, drug profits will collapse—and with them, the drug empires.

I am not advocating no laws at all regulating drugs, no governmental restraints on sales to minors, no quality controls to curtail overdose, and no prosecution of the inevitable bootleggers. Legalization, by contrast, means that the government would maintain regulatory control over drug sales, possibly through state clinics or stores. It would be the task of the Food and Drug Administration to guarantee purity and safety, as it does for alcoholic beverages. Shooting up would be outlawed in public, just as drinking liquor is. Advertising would be strictly prohibited, selling drugs to children would continue to be a criminal offense, and other evasions of government regulations would be prosecuted. Driving, flying, or piloting a vessel under the influence would still be punished. Taxes on drugs would pay for enforcement, education, rehabilitation, and research (a net benefit is estimated of at least $10 billion from reduced expenditures on enforcement and new tax revenues).

Legalization would lead to an immediate decrease in murders, burglaries, and robberies, paralleling the end of alcohol prohibition in 1933—though the spread of powerful weapons in U.S. society and the proliferation of youth gangs has led to an addiction to gun violence that will not soon go away. Cheap drugs would mean that most addicts would not be driven to crime to support their habit, and that drug lords would no longer have a turf to

> *"Legalization . . . means that the government would maintain regulatory control over drug sales, possibly through state clinics or stores."*

fight over. Legalization would force South American peasants to switch back to less lucrative crops; but that would be less devastating than destruction of their crops altogether by aerial spraying or biological warfare. Legalization would enable countries like Colombia, Bolivia, and Peru to regularize the cocaine sector and absorb its money-making capacity into the taxable, legal, unionized economic world. Legalization would be a blow to dealers, who would be deprived of their ticket to riches. It would remove glamorous Al Capone–type traffickers who are role-models for the young, and it would destroy the "cool" status of drug use. But it would leave us with a monolithic problem: how to provide decent jobs for unemployed youths. Indeed, until the root economic factors that contribute to drug use are addressed, drug addiction will continue.

Drug legalization would cancel the corrupting role of the drug cartels in South American politics, a powerful incentive to corruption at all levels of our own government, and a dangerous threat to our civil liberties through mistaken enforcement and property confiscation. It would free law enforcement agencies to focus on other crimes and reduce the strain on the court and prison systems. It would scuttle a multibillion dollar bureaucracy whose prosperity depends on *not* solving the drug problem. It would remove a major cause of public cynicism about obeying the laws of the land. It could help check the spread of AIDS and hepatitis through a free supply of hypodermic needles.

Legalization would also free up money wasted on interdiction of illicit drugs that is desperately needed for treatment, education, and research.

Legalization: The Risks

The worst prospect is that legalization might lead to a short-term increase in the use of drugs due to easier availability, lower prices, and the sudden freedom from prosecution. The repeal of Prohibition seems to have had that result, then alcohol use gradually declined. Drugs cheap enough to destroy their profitability would also be in the range of any schoolchild's allowance, just like beer and cigarettes. Cocaine is easily concealable and its effects less overt than alcohol. The possibility of increased teenage use is admittedly frightening.

On the other hand, ending the drug war would free drug control officers to concentrate on protecting children from exploitation, and here stiff penalties would continue to be in effect. The alarmist prediction that cheap, available drugs could lead to an addiction rate of 75 percent of regular users simply ignores the fact that 95 percent of people in the United States are already using some form of drugs when nicotine, caffeine, alcohol, and prescription drugs are included. We can learn from the mistakes made with the repeal of Prohibition, when the lid was simply removed with virtually no education or restriction on advertising and little government regulation. A major educational program would need to be in effect well before drug legalization took effect. Anti-alcohol and anti-tobacco ad campaigns have already proven effective in restricting use. In Canada, for example, cigarettes sell for about three times the U.S. price, and vigorous campaigns against smoking have had some success, especially among the young.

Decriminalization

We already have some evidence that legalization works. In the 11 U.S. states that briefly "decriminalized" marijuana in the 1970s, the number of users stayed about the same. In the Netherlands, legal tolerance of marijuana and hashish has led to a significant *decline* in consumption and has successfully prevented kids from experimenting with hard drugs. Eleven times as many U.S. high school seniors smoked pot daily in 1983 as did students the same age in the Netherlands. The Dutch discovered that making the purchase of small amounts of marijuana freely available to anyone over 16 cuts the drug dealer out; as a result, there is virtually no crime associated with the use of marijuana. Treatment

> *"In the Netherlands, legal tolerance of marijuana and hashish has led to a significant decline in consumption."*

for addiction to hard drugs is widely available there; 75 percent of the heroin addicts in Amsterdam are on methadone maintenance, living relatively normal, crime-free lives. Since the needle exchange program was first introduced in the mid-1980s, the HIV infection rate among injecting drug users in cities like Amsterdam has dropped from 11 percent to 4 percent and is now one of the lowest in the world. All this still falls short of legalization, and problems still abound, but the experience of the Netherlands clearly points in the right direction. The Dutch see illicit drug use as a health problem, not as a criminal problem.

> *"A nonviolent, nonreactive, creative approach is needed that lets the drug empire collapse of its own deadly weight."*

Just an Illusion

Fighting the drug war may appear to hold the high moral ground, but this is only an illusion; in fact it increases the damage drugs do to the whole society by making it so lucrative. Some have argued that legalization would legitimate or place the state's moral imprimatur on drugs, but we have already legalized the most lethal drugs, and no one argues that this constitutes governmental endorsement. Sale of Valium, alcohol, cigarettes, pesticides, and poisons are all permitted and regulated by the state, without anyone assuming that the state encourages their use. Legalization would indeed imply that drugs are no longer being satanized, like "demon rum."

Some people argue that legalization represents a daring and risky experiment, but it is prohibition that is the daring and risky experiment, argues drug researcher Jonathan Ott. Inebriating drugs have been mostly legal throughout the millennia of human existence. The drastic step was taken in the second decade of the twentieth century in the United States when for the first time large-scale, comprehensive legal control of inebriating drugs was implemented. It is safe to say after decades of federal control of inebriating drugs that the experiment has been a dismal and costly failure. Human and animal use of inebriants is as natural as any other aspect of social behavior; it is the attempt to crush this normal drive that is bizarre and unnatural. Already 95 percent of our adult population is using drugs, and the vast majority do so responsibly. Most people who would misuse drugs are already doing so. Public attitudes have swung against drunkenness and driving while intoxicated; now anti-smoking sentiments are burgeoning. We have every reason to believe that the public will continue to censure addiction to drugs.

A Nonviolent Approach

No one wants to live in a country overrun with drugs, but we already do. We should at the very least commit ourselves to a policy of "harm reduction." We cannot stop drug violence with state violence. Addicts will be healed by care and compassion, not condemnation. Dealers will be curbed by a ruined world drug market, not by enforcement that simply escalates the profitability of drugs. A nonviolent, nonreactive, creative approach is needed that lets the drug empire collapse of its own deadly weight.

We have been letting our violent resistance to drugs beget the very thing we seek to destroy. When our nonviolent Quaker tradition offers an alternative to our failed drug war, shouldn't we consider trying it?

Legalizing Drugs Would Reduce Crime

by Steven B. Duke

About the author: *Steven B. Duke is a Yale law professor and the coauthor, with Albert C. Gross, of* America's Longest War: Rethinking Our Tragic Crusade Against Drugs, *published by Jeremy P. Tarcher/Putnam.*

In her assertion that legalizing drugs would markedly reduce crime, [former U.S. surgeon general] Dr. Joycelyn Elders was clearly correct. Given the enormity of the nation's crime problem, her suggestion that legalization should be "studied" was also plainly right. In asserting that the matter should not even be thought about, the Bill Clinton Administration behaved like religious rulers decrying heresy. What should be embarrassing to an Administration elected on a promise of "change" is not what its surgeon general said, but her White House colleagues' contemptuous dismissal of what she said.

Beyond Dispute

That drug prohibition is responsible for much of the crime in this country is beyond dispute. In terms of crime rates, the most serious mistake America ever made was to limit its repeal of Prohibition to a single drug—alcohol, the only drug that commonly triggers violent propensities in its users. Had we fully repealed drug prohibition in 1933, our crime rates today would be no more than half what they now are.

Property crime rates have tripled and violent crime rates have doubled since President Richard M. Nixon created the Drug Enforcement Agency in 1973 and declared an "all-out global war" to end the "drug menace." The connection is not coincidental.

The more effective are law-enforcement efforts against drug distribution, the more costly the drugs become to their consumers. After a generation of escalating drug war efforts, the costs of marijuana, cocaine and heroin are about 100 times what they would be in a free market. The inevitable effect of jacking up the cost of drugs is the commission of crime by drug users to obtain money to buy drugs.

From Steven B. Duke, "How Legalization Would Cut Crime," *Los Angeles Times*, December 21, 1993. Reprinted with permission of the author.

In a survey of persons in prison for robbery or burglary, one out of three said that they committed their crimes in order to buy drugs. In a survey of adolescents, those who admitted using cocaine, 1.3%, accounted for 49% of the admitted crimes. In several studies of prisoners, 65% to 80% have admitted regular or lifetime illicit drug use. About 75% of our robberies, thefts, burglaries and related assaults are committed by drug abusers. Numerous studies show that drug users commit far fewer crimes when undergoing outpatient drug therapy or even when the price of drugs drops.

The Drug Trade and Crime

Creating incentives to steal and rob to buy drugs is not the only crime-inducing effect of prohibition, perhaps not even the main one. Murder and assault are employed to protect or acquire drug-selling turf, to settle disputes among drug merchants and their customers, to steal drugs or drug money from dealers. In major cities, at least one-fourth of the killings are systemic to the drug trade. The victims of internecine drug warfare are often innocent bystanders, even infants and school-children.

Drug prohibition also accounts for much of the proliferation of handguns. Drug dealers must enforce their own contracts and provide their own protection from predators; even "mules" who deliver drugs need weapons. Packing a gun, like fancy clothing or gold jewelry, has become a status symbol among many adolescents. In such an atmosphere, other youngsters carry guns for—they hope—protection. A decade ago, only 15% of teenagers

> *"The inevitable effect of jacking up the cost of drugs is the commission of crime by drug users to obtain money to buy drugs."*

who got into serious trouble in New York City were carrying guns, now the rate is 60%–65%.

The drug trade and the crime and violence attached to it take place mainly in our cities, rendering whole neighborhoods unfit for human habitation. As the rot spreads, even more crime is generated by the climate of disorder and ennui it produces.

Drug prohibition also fosters crime by producing official corruption. The news media are full of accounts of cops caught stealing money or drugs from dealers or simply taking money to look the other way. Even judges and prosecutors are sometimes implicated. Such pervasive corruption denigrates and demoralizes all law enforcers and causes disrespect for law among citizens.

Adverse Effects of the Drug War

The distractive effects of the drug war on law enforcement indirectly but profoundly encourage crime. In many cities, half or more of arrests are for drugs or related crimes, expending police resources and energy that might otherwise be available for domestic violence, fraud and other serious offenses. As a consequence, all criminals have a much better chance of escaping detection and punishment than if drugs were legal.

The drug war also deeply undercuts the role of incarceration in dealing with people convicted of such serious crimes as child molesting, rape, kidnaping and homicide. There is no room in our prisons: 40 states are under court orders for overcrowding. Funds are not available to build prisons fast enough to provide the needed space. Violent criminals are being paroled early or are having their sentences chopped to make space for drug users and dealers.

> *"All criminals have a much better chance of escaping detection and punishment than if drugs were legal."*

The drug war (excluding treatment and preventive education expenditures) costs about $9 billion at the federal level and about twice that on the state and local levels. These estimates do not count the law-enforcement cost chargeable to crimes that are prohibition-caused but not technically drug-related—probably another $15 billion at all levels of government. Thus, law-enforcement costs attributable to the drug war are at least $40 billion per year. The losses to crime victims in property alone (not counting lives lost or bodies maimed) are probably another $10 billion. In addition, the drug war imposes a premium of at least $50 billion on the price of drugs and the cost to drug consumers. The total annual costs of the drug war, therefore, are about $100 billion. If drugs were legalized, most of this money could be spent on long-term crime prevention.

Many Benefits

Legalizing drugs would not be cost free. We could expect somewhat more use of presently illicit drugs and, all other things remaining the same, more drug abuse. But things would not remain the same. Vast sums would be freed for prevention and treatment of drug abuse and for reducing its root causes. Among the many other benefits of legalization would be the reduction of AIDS and other diseases transmitted by drug abusers, less risk of drug overdose or poisoning, better prenatal care for pregnant women with drug problems and restoration of our civil liberties, to name a few.

How the law should treat the distribution and consumption of psychoactive drugs is an issue on which reasonable people can differ. There is, however, no room to doubt that legalizing such drugs would greatly reduce our crime rates. Everyone familiar with the crime problem knows that no bill pending in Congress and no other anti-crime measure proposed by anyone has the slightest chance of substantially reducing the ravages of crime.

A society that regards crime as one of its greatest problems yet allows its leaders to refuse to consider the only known solution, deserves the leaders—and crime—it gets.

Proposals to Legalize Drugs Merit Consideration

by Fred Reed

About the author: *Fred Reed writes the "Police Beat" column for the* Washington Times *daily newspaper.*

I

The possibility of legalizing drugs continues to arise, often in respectable circles. Maybe we ought to think about it.

When the idea comes up, many people seem to believe that complete legalization is envisioned, so that anyone could buy cocaine at the convenience store, like milk.

New Addicts

Almost everyone's response is that the consequence would be the creation of millions of new addicts. Countless people would be willing to try drugs, the reasoning goes, since it would be both legal and safe. Many would become addicted, as doctors do now, simply because of easy availability.

I suspect that this is exactly what would happen. What many advocates of legality have in mind, however, is quite different. Many schemes exist.

Most involve having addicts register with, say, federal clinics or the equivalent. The junkie would receive his drugs, and perhaps have to administer them at the clinic. Since few middle-class folk would want to try drugs badly enough to register, new addiction would not be encouraged.

Again, there are variations proposed to overcome objections.

An Enormous Toll

Good idea, or bad?

The "pro" side of the question is straightforward. Drugs exact an enormous toll on society. Few people, I think, know just how enormous. The jails are jammed with drug offenders, the morgues with young (mostly black) males

From Fred Reed, "Legalization of Some Drugs Is Worth a Try," *Washington Times*, April 29, 1996, and "Drug Legalization Beats Other Strategies," *Washington Times*, June 10, 1996. Reprinted by permission of the *Washington Times*.

killed in the drug wars, the courts with backlogs of drug cases.

More threatening to most of us is that the high rates of violent robbery, as well as burglary and shoplifting, spring in large part from the need of addicts to buy drugs. Police spend man-years on chasing petty users and peddlers. They have other things to do.

The effect on race relations is grim, and this we don't need. The attempt to stop the flow of drugs puts police in what amounts to a state of war against blacks.

> *"We can't stop the tide of drugs as long as their sale is so very profitable."*

If you don't think so, spend some time downtown in a police car, or in the courts. Whites use drugs, but they don't die by hundreds in drug-war drive-bys. Blacks in the bad sections of cities have enough problems without drugs and killings.

Further, we can't stop the tide of drugs as long as their sale is so very profitable.

A Lost War

If there was a war on drugs, we lost it long ago. The politicians will lie about this when it is to their advantage to do so, but go look on the streets.

Look at the endless clusters of dealers in the bad sections, and in the not-so-bad sections. Look at the unbelievable markup on drugs from South American field to American street, look at the difficulty of sealing thousands of miles of coastline and all of our airspace, and you will see that it isn't doable.

No shiny new program just like all the rest, no heartwarming optimistic speech from the president is going to make the slightest difference. And presidents know it.

Finally, although many would viscerally disagree, drugs are not evil in the sense that, say, molesting children is evil.

Drugs can destroy lives, as alcohol can. Arguably, since addicts are going to get their drugs anyway, it is better to let them do it without engaging in crime to pay for their habits. So, at any rate, the advocates believe. And since we can't win anyway, we might as well try legalization.

Effects of Legalization

What would the effects be? I don't know that anyone is entirely sure.

It seems to me that the huge market for illegal drugs would vanish overnight, along with the crime needed to support habits.

I suspect that the appalling proportion of young blacks currently entangled in the system of criminal justice would drop very sharply indeed, as would the number of homicides, again chiefly among young blacks and Hispanics. The population of the prisons would drop fast.

On the other hand, the effect might be to let society forget about the underclass entirely.

119

Some (I may be one) might suspect legalization of being a convenient way to keep troublesome minorities doped up while eliminating the crime that is the main reason why people in Bethesda [a Maryland suburb of Washington, D.C.] ever think about what goes on downtown.

At best, legalization might take enough pressure off susceptible populations to allow underlying problems to be addressed.

Maybe, just maybe, if the drug traffic didn't provide such a lucrative temptation to the enterprising in Anacostia [a Washington, D.C., community], school and real jobs might look a lot more attractive. Maybe not.

But what we are doing now isn't working, and isn't going to work. Maybe the experiment is worth trying somewhere, just to see what would happen.

II

Some time ago, I wrote a column suggesting that controlled legalization of drugs might be a reasonable idea [see part I]. Since then, I have been living on the run. OK, I haven't actually had anyone try to lynch me, but several cops I know have strongly suggested it isn't a good idea.

I don't think it's a good idea myself. I do, however, wonder whether it isn't the best idea available. Maybe not. But I'll tell you why I wonder.

Whenever the idea arises, those against it—who, by the way, are perfectly good, sane people—always say it wouldn't work and then offer what they think would be a workable solution to the drug problem. Trouble is, I don't think any of their suggestions would do the job. Let's look at a few.

Unworkable Solutions

One substitute for legalization I hear is the hard-nosed approach: more cops, more prisons, longer sentences, less parole. The rationale is that drugs are criminal, and we've just got to do what's necessary to show these people they can't get away with it. Slam-dunk them. Make them wish they hadn't been born.

I don't think this one will work. Sure, if we got *really* hard-nosed—if we imposed a police state—we could wipe drugs out. Easily. Just allow warrantless searches and shoot on the sidewalk anyone found with drugs.

The practical problem (never mind the moral problem) is that the country is nearing the limit of its willingness to spend and punish. Or I think it is, anyway. Few want to pay for tripling police forces, building and

> *"At best, legalization might take enough pressure off susceptible populations to allow underlying problems to be addressed."*

operating several times more prisons, throwing ever-larger numbers of people in jail for small amounts of dope.

Further, the jail-them-all approach ignores the racial aspect of drugs. Those jailed are very heavily black. Most of them haven't done anything to deserve sentences more fitting for murder, rape and armed robbery. Someday something is going to blow. We had better be careful on this one.

The Military and Drug Education

A related solution is to use the military to keep drugs out of the country. As one cop recently said to me, "You mean to tell me the armed forces can't control the borders of the country?" Yeah, that's exactly what I mean.

People who say "use the military" haven't looked at a radar screen of the boat and plane traffic into the United States. It's incredible. Try multiplying the time to thoroughly search a sizable boat by the number of boats to be searched.

> *"The jail-them-all approach ignores the racial aspect of drugs. Those jailed are very heavily black."*

Heavy sentences won't work. The boat drivers are expendables. It flatly isn't possible, even without the Constitution. The profits are so phenomenal that catching even most of the incoming drugs wouldn't stop it.

Another solution is rehabilitation, perhaps combined with education, jobs and social services. This amounts to saying that if we solve all our social problems, no one will want drugs. Right. Any day now.

It is stupefyingly obvious that we are not going to spend the money that would be needed to improve rehabilitation efforts. There are better reasons than drugs for improving education, and we don't do it. The jobs aren't there and aren't going to be. Rehabilitation is an outright scam in places like Washington. At best, it helps a few at a price prohibitive for large populations. There is zero chance that huge sums will become available to rehab South Chicago.

Another solution is programs to persuade people not to want drugs. You know, DARE [Drug Abuse Resistance Education] in the schools, consciousness-raising, self-esteem work. These appeal to nice, middle-class, white people who don't have a clue how things work in drug-using populations, white or black.

Whether it's white crackers in the bush of Florida or blacks in the projects of Newark, things are bad enough for them that propaganda from culturally alien do-good missionaries from suburbia isn't going to do squat.

Maybe these programs self-actualize the missionaries, and they certainly put salaries in a massive number of pockets. Neither is what is needed.

No, controlled legalization isn't the perfect answer, nor is it even a good answer. In fact, it's an appalling idea. But, got a better one? I mean, one that will work? Or might work? Proposing impossible solutions is easy and perhaps satisfying. What good does it do?

Drugs are eating the cities alive, leading directly to horrendous rates of murder, setting entire populations against the rest of society. Unless someone comes up with a politically possible solution, and I haven't heard one, I claim it's not crazy to think about it.

Marijuana Should Be Legalized

by Matt McGrath

About the author: *Matt McGrath is an engineering graduate of Tufts University in Medford, Massachusetts.*

One of the best known plants on Earth is cannabis. It has been a part of civilizations for thousands of years, in one form or another. It has been most widely used in history under another name, hemp. The hemp plant yields very strong fibers that can be used to make fabric and paper and yields seeds that are very high in protein. For hundreds of years, the plant was harvested in many parts of the world to supply these basic needs. It was one of the first crops planted in the new world and was harvested by many of the founding fathers. In some strains of the plant—cannabis sativa and more commonly, cannabis indica—the flowering buds were harvested and processed to remove a resin, or hashish, that was smoked and ingested by poets, writers, and the aristocracy. It is this resin that is still a part of the world's economy today. The rest of the plant is no longer a necessity since the creation of synthetic fibers like nylon and rayon. Due to the resin that this plant produces, it holds a special place in the world of trade. It is a rare item that commands a relatively high price and is not subject to taxation. It enjoys these conditions because it is illegal.

The Path to Prohibition

Obviously the plant has not always been illegal; otherwise it could not have been used so widely, from clothing the settlers to supplying the paper for the Gutenberg Bible. The push to make cannabis illegal came in the mid to late 30's. At that time, the U.S. Agriculture Department had been pushing to switch paper production from trees to hemp, since it would help ease the problem of possible deforestation. In 1936, a machine was finally built that could separate the pulp and the fiber in a cost effective manner. Yet at this same time, a group of companies, among them DuPont Chemicals, Hearst Paper and Timber, and several other industrial giants, had developed a new method to produce whiter

From Matt McGrath, "Economic Considerations on the Legalization of Cannabis" (December 13, 1994), www.tufts.edu/~mmcgrath/econ.html, July 30, 1997. Reprinted by permission of the author.

paper. They had invested a lot of capital in this project, and if the cheaper hemp was going to be used, they all stood to lose a considerable amount of money. These big businesses had many government connections, were very powerful, and in the case of Hearst, owned a newspaper chain. They decided that to save their investment, they were going to exploit one of the properties of the cannabis plant: The fact that when smoked, the resin would produce a sensation of euphoria.

This attribute of the plant was not well known by most of the American public, so Hearst began a disinformation campaign. He used a Mexican slang term for the plant, "marijuana," thereby associating the plant that so many farmers had grown for years as a Mexican "devil weed." He claimed through stories in his papers that smoking the plant would turn people into "axe wielding murderers." Since there was a good degree of distrust of Mexicans in general at the time, it was easy to convince the public that the plant was horrible and should be eradicated. This campaign brought about the 1937 Marijuana Tax Act, which effectively made marijuana illegal, despite emotional protest from the American Medical Association, which was very interested in its many valuable medicinal properties. Although hemp was briefly legalized during World War II, accompanied by the government propaganda film *Hemp for Victory*, the need for additional industrial fiber passed, and it was once again made a controlled substance.

Effects of Marijuana

Many people don't understand exactly what is happening when a person smokes cannabis and gets "high." When a person smokes the plant, a chemical called Delta-9-Tetrahydrocarbinol (or, more commonly, THC) is released and absorbed into the bloodstream through the lungs. Once in the bloodstream, it breaks down into metabolites that travel to the brain, where they take the place of certain normally occurring chemicals. These imitation chemicals are slightly different and thereby affect the brain cells differently, yet without causing any cellular damage whatsoever. After a while, they are washed out by the natural elements, and the sensation of being "high" or "stoned" is lost. This euphoria begins slightly like alcohol intoxication but is much smoother and does not cloud the head like alcohol. It makes sensations seem more intense, and emotions are enhanced. It also produces no hangover and is flushed naturally out of the body over a period of time.

> *"[Marijuana] produces no hangover and is flushed naturally out of the body over a period of time."*

THC is actually an extremely mild hallucinogen, and in large quantities it can produce very slight visual phenomena. This is not experienced by all users, and very few try to achieve this state.

Currently, cannabis is a Schedule I drug, meaning that it has no accepted medical uses. This classification is questionable if for no other reason than the fact that the American Medical Association, during the eleventh hour of the ratification of the Marijuana Tax Act, fought vehemently for access to the plant for medicinal purposes. The prohibition of this drug is quite expensive to maintain. The government seeks to attain this goal on several levels. It prosecutes dealers and users, it eradicates crops both within and outside this country, and it attempts to "teach" the public about the drug. These are all very noble efforts, but they are not working the way they are designed to.

The War on Marijuana

There has been a recent upsurge in the number of cannabis-related arrests as the drug has made a resurgence among the public. Its current popularity is much greater than at its coming out in the Sixties, as it is no longer just the drug of the counter-culture. But today's crusade against the drug does hearken back to that of President Richard Nixon's. Law enforcement officials are spending a great deal of taxpayers' money to fight this drug. They are making more arrests, more raids, and more seizures than ever before. Yet the problem still persists. Helicopters equipped with heat-sensitive scanning equipment fly over houses, looking for abnormal heat sources, where maybe someone has an indoor growing room. Even if they do have an indoor growing room, that's not reason to assume that they're growing pot. This assumption has very frequently led to misdirected searches and needless intrusion into private homes in the name of morality. Apologies for these sorts of "mistakes" are kept very quiet, and because it is often the word of the victim against that of a police officer, it is very difficult to win a lawsuit for mental anguish on behalf of the citizen.

> *"If the number of people who smoke marijuana . . . continues to increase, there are going to be more convicts than free men."*

Once these arrests are made, the criminals must be held and prosecuted. But because of the volume of these arrests, jail space is running out, and courtrooms are backed up for months. This clearly is a violation of the criminal's constitutional right to a fair and speedy trial. Even the trials aren't that fair anymore. There is a new type of sentencing called "mandatory minimums" that has been enacted to "aid" the judge in the determination of a sentence. This minimum rule is in the form of a chart, which equates the possession of illegal substances in varying quantities with varying jail sentences. This set of rules, which the judge is legally bound to follow takes the case out of his hands and places it in those of a group of legislators, who have no idea of the peculiarities of the case at hand. The only discretion the judge is given is whether or not he would like to raise the sentence. This is infuriating to judges who would like to lessen the penalty but can't. As they should, some have stood up to this lunacy and handed down lighter punishments, despite the repercussions they might face themselves.

Once sentenced, the criminal must be housed somewhere, and this is causing a huge boom in prison population. The National Institute of Drug Abuse released findings that over three-fourths of all drug-related arrests made each year are for marijuana. This is space taken up by people who have committed what are almost always non-violent crimes. This mandatory sentencing is putting thieves and murderers back out on the streets quicker than those who are only hurting themselves. Prison overcrowding is becoming a serious problem, and the War on Drugs has not yet justified its contribution to the problem. If the number of people who smoke marijuana (now estimated conservatively at 25 million) continues to increase, there are going to be more convicts than free men. These are also laws that are taking the responsibility for one's self from the people and putting it in the hands of the state, thereby stripping the person of the power over their own body. . . .

Telling the Truth

Many of the problems that have been discussed here can be either solved or lessened by simply legalizing the drug. This would be the biggest change in the economy since the end of prohibition. This notion is a shock to most people, since they have always been lectured to about the evils of drugs, but it really is a very sound choice. Before any of the laws can be changed, though, the public would have to be told the truth. This would require a slight admission by the government that maybe not everything that they had told the public was true— unfortunately, this is not a strong point of our elected officials. Once the public had been reeducated as to the truths and myths of marijuana consumption, the work could begin on the cultivation, distribution, and uses of cannabis.

Growing Cannabis

To grow cannabis would be very simple for any farmer. The plant is in essence a weed that grows very well, despite climate and soil, and can be made to grow in all fifty states. Indoor growing can naturally be used, but this would really only be feasible in cultivating exotic indica strains that are high in THC and require specific nutrients and environmental attention to flourish. Harvesting of the hemp would not be a problem, since the machinery to do so has been around for a long time. The farmers would now have a new crop option, but there would still have to be some control initially as to who is allowed to cultivate the plant, since the market has never before been tested to determine how much it can handle. A set amount of cannabis should be cultivated and put on the market so that farmers do not

> *"Marijuana is less damaging to children than alcohol."*

devote too much of their land to growing it. Once the demand has been estimated, more farmers can be allowed to grow the plant, and prices will begin to adjust as the product becomes more commonplace. In addition to consumable cannabis, industrial hemp can also be grown. The industrial hemp can be genetically engineered to reduce the THC content to almost zero, while the fibers remain unaffected. This hemp can be used in textiles, food, and biomass fuels, saving money in the long run, after the initial changeover cost of some of the machinery. Although the fields of the consumable cannabis might be better off with a fence to guard against thieves, the theft of plants should be relatively small as time passes, since a processed product would be available at a reasonable price. And processing of the product would also be very simple. The machines that now process tobacco could be used to chop up the plants. Once the buds and leaves have been removed from the stem, the chopped plant matter could be dried and rolled. No additives would be needed, since smokers really don't need any. Taste and freshness additives are unnecessary.

> *"The idea of revenue from cannabis taxation should thrill the government."*

Distribution and Pricing

Distribution of the cannabis is a very touchy issue, since this substance is definitely not for children. There would have to be government regulation, exactly like that of alcohol, abiding by the 21-year-age limit, and the primary use of pharmacies as distribution points. The critics will say that the legal drinking age has not stopped underage drinking, and the same logic can be applied to marijuana regulation. Although this is completely true, it can also be shown that marijuana is less damaging to children than alcohol, so the concern is slightly countered by the comparison of the effects of the two substances being examined. Prices would also have to be established. At first, prices would be relatively high (yet lower than street prices) while the market is tested out. These high prices account for the initial cost of harvest and the uncertainty of the consumer market. Once companies establish their production lines, the prices will become standard, which could be estimated, based on street prices, to be about double that of a pack of tobacco cigarettes. That price estimation is taking into account that the price will drop once the black market has been eliminated. Pharmacies are also the logical choice for the sale of the high quality strains of indica. The purity of these strains is very important to the marijuana connoisseur, and to have a choice of exotic strains, such as Northern Lights, Chocolate Thai, and Purple Haze, aficionados can be absolutely sure of what they are buying. Even the more commercial strains of cannabis, the sativas, could be sold in loose quantities so that people could roll their own cigarettes and pack pipes instead of buying the prepackaged brands. Hashish, which is more of a specialty item among smokers, could also be produced and sold. The resin extraction process would be expensive to initiate, but once the market got on its feet, the introduction of such an aristocratic product should be profitable. Finally, seeds could be sold, but this is a more tricky market. If one can cultivate the plant, then they have no use for the commercial brands, so the seeds must be expensive. Also, the seeds must have a high growth potential, based on their price. The demand for seeds would probably not be overwhelming enough to drive out the commercial cannabis market, though, since there is a serious investment for growing supplies.

New Taxes

The driving force behind all of this is, as always, money. Specifically, who gets it. The consumers are going to feel the bite here, and it's going to come in the form of taxes. The idea of revenue from cannabis taxation should thrill the government. Hypothetically speaking, if the number of smokers is conservatively estimated at 25 million, and they very conservatively spend 200 dollars a year on cannabis that is taxed at the special rate of 10%, that's 750 million dollars in taxes. These numbers—except for the tax, which is high, though not unreasonable based on cigarette taxes—are on the low side. The tax revenues from this market are staggering. These taxes are only the beginning, though, since money will be saved through prison population reductions and law enforcement reductions. There is even the chance that the market can be opened up to international trade with the Netherlands, to keep the market internationally competitive.

Workplace Issues

Now of course we must ask ourselves, how is this new freedom going to hurt people? Well, there will be some damage done, but it is far less severe than the money that is now being wasted on the War on Drugs. If cannabis were to be legalized, there would be a loss of money in some fields, while others would obviously flourish. The first rallying cry of the anti-drug advocate is "lost productivity in the workplace." This is unfortunately true, as some people will abuse their new freedom. The workplace is definitely no place to be high, as most competent workers know. It is certainly possible, though, with easy access to pot, that people who think that they can function normally while high will try to go to work high. This can exact a high price should the driver of a bus, train, or airplane report to work high. This leads to the cost of a system to test and make sure that no public servant, or anyone who holds the lives of others in their hands, can work while under an influence. Although cannabis produces no hangover effects after use, a person can still feel unmotivated if they consume too much, and this amotivation can definitely slow down a workplace.

> *"Cannabis is not strongly addictive like nicotine."*

There is also the option of companies to institute, as many do now, mandatory drug testing. Although this is often called an invasion of privacy, it would probably be a good investment in fields that require attention to minute detail and high responsibility. But even for these positions, a new type of drug test should be researched to determine how long ago the person was last under an influence. Current tests only show that a person smoked within the last 28 days, which is scientifically useless information. It makes no sense to penalize a person applying for a job who got high the week before. As long as they do not smoke while they are accountable for their work, they should not be refused employment.

Loss of Profits

Other casualties of legalization would be the tobacco and alcohol industries. With another mood-altering drug on the market, their profits would decrease proportionally. This is also a prime reason that moguls such as Philip Morris and Anheuser-Busch donate hundreds of thousands of dollars each year to anti-drug campaigns. They know what they stand to lose. Although tobacco plants could easily convert to cannabis processing, they have no real desire to, since cannabis is not strongly addictive like nicotine. The cigarettes keep the people coming back at an alarming rate, and the cannabis would not. Alcohol, a poison, is able to produce some of the sensations of being high, but after a certain level, it simply makes a person sick, dehydrates them, and kills brain cells by oxygen deprivation. It is also addictive in some instances. Again, cannabis, which produces a much "cleaner" and more clearheaded experience, is preferable to alcohol. The two can be combined, but this is not very safe, as a human who is high can consume more alcohol than a normal person, which is potentially harmful. The pot also enhances the feeling of drunkenness, so a small amount of pot and a few beers is equal to lots of beers. Thus consumption rates would drop among people who mix their substances. Alcohol would bear a much bigger loss than tobacco, simply because cannabis acts so much like alcohol, but with more pleasant mental effects and no hangover. A partial solution to this problem would be to market a cannabis drink. THC is soluble in alcohol, but not in water, so a good place to start would be a stout beer with THC extract in it.

> *"The damage done by pot smoke is still less than that done by tobacco smoke."*

Impact on Health

The final cost that would be incurred by the people would be their physical health. The smoking of any plant matter does considerable damage to one's lungs. But there are two solutions to this problem. The first is simply to eat the pot instead of smoking it. The reason this is not done on a large scale now is because the amount of pot needed to produce a high when eaten is almost double what is needed when smoked. But when the prices drop with legalization, it would not be as expensive. The second alternative is the use of water pipes. A water pipe filters the smoke through a vessel of water. As the smoke passes through the water, many carcinogens are trapped in the water, but since THC is not water soluble, nothing is lost from the smoke. This method also cools the smoke, which is better for the lungs. But the sale of water pipes in the U.S. became a crime January 1, 1995. The damage done by pot smoke is still less than that done by tobacco smoke. Nicotine hardens the arteries and increases blood pressure, but THC does nothing of the sort. In its pure form, THC is actually a bronchial dilator, meaning that when ingested, it opens up airways, allowing dirt and phlegm to be expelled more easily. Most cannabis today is also higher in tar content

> *"Cannabis has been determined to be very beneficial to terminally ill patients in easing their pain."*

than cigarettes, but once legalized, the buds of the plant, which are low in tar, would be more common, and thus tar intake would not be as high. There would also be some mental health problems. Although pot is not physically addictive, in some people it can become mentally addictive, to the point where they can't enjoy themselves unless they're high. This is an extreme case, but it does happen. Treatment for these people would be costly, as they would have to be shown that they can operate without cannabis. This craving cycle is also broken in most people after about a month of abstinence, but its success naturally goes hand in hand with a person's own willpower. Treatment programs much like Alcoholics Anonymous or Narcotics Anonymous could be instituted to help people deal with their mental instabilities in a group setting. Health care would also have to be modified to handle any treatment needed. But legalization should not necessarily increase premiums, either. Addictive personalities occur in about 15% of the population, so to assume that a pot smoker is going to have a problem is unreasonable.

A major concern with legalization is the operation of motor vehicles. No one should operate a motor vehicle under any influence, especially cannabis. Currently, alcohol is the biggest factor in highway accidents and fatalities. Pot and other drugs account for only about 8% of these accidents, although with wider availability, this number could rise. The only way to combat this problem is through education, as is now employed in dealing with drunk driving. People must be made aware, and the cost of doing so is a minor supplement to current campaigns. "Don't drink and drive" can be printed simultaneously with "Get high, get a ride" or some similar catch phrase. For this reason, auto insurance would probably increase at the onset of legalization for fear of an increase in accidents. The only way to fight this is through education, which is less costly than the lives it can save.

Medical Marijuana

One last industry that has nothing to gain and much to lose from legalization are the pharmaceuticals manufacturers. Cannabis has been determined to be very beneficial to terminally ill patients in easing their pain. Some glaucoma patients have had access to pure THC drops for their eyes, which made them feel much better. Currently chemotherapy and AIDS patients are seeking access to the plant to increase their appetite and counter their nausea long enough to hold down a solid meal. But even for these terminally ill patients, cannabis has not been used, as it is still Schedule I. There is a substitute, Marinol, which is a type of THC extract, but it is more difficult to titrate than smoking and does not produce a very pleasant sensation in the body. It is believed that other chemicals found in the plant apart from THC are responsible for some of the medicinal attributes of the plant. But if cannabis were to be legalized, the pharmaceutical companies could not make a sizable profit since they cannot patent a plant. It's in their best interest to produce expensive chemical substitutes. If a patient wants to use marijuana medically, he must find it himself, risking arrest, and cannot be compensated by medical insurance for its purchase. It is appalling to think that the medical moguls are so interested in money to lose sight of their responsibilities to serve their patients to the best of their knowledge.

There are many arguments other than the ones presented in this viewpoint both for and against legalization. Many of the proponents of prohibition are stuck in what they feel to be their moral obligations, but their War on Drugs is only a waste of their money. They can't seem to realize that legalization of cannabis is not going to bring the world as they know it to an end, but rather it will be better for almost everyone. The current roadblock in educating the public is the fact that the government will not reverse its stance

> *"People must be made to realize what a waste prohibition is and that the economy would greatly benefit from legal and taxable marijuana."*

on the dangers of cannabis. People must be made to realize what a waste prohibition is and that the economy would greatly benefit from legal and taxable marijuana. There are going to be some rather hefty transition costs to be dealt with, but after the initial introduction, the investment in harvesting and packaging machinery, production of smoking paraphernalia, and menu costs for all affected industries will be offset on the large scale by public consumption and reductions in the spending on the War on Drugs. Right now, the first step that should be made is in the field of medical marijuana. Its use by ill patients would set an example of how cannabis is a medicinal drug, the first step to remove it from its Schedule I classification. Currently, support for marijuana legalization is costly to the character of elected officials, but if enough people are made aware of the truths, they can lower the cost of support and bring this issue into national debate, devoid of myths and urban legend. The investment in the fight for legalization is high and risky at present, but the promise of a tremendous return should be enough to convince anyone of its economic legitimacy.

Illegal Drugs Should Not Be Legalized

by Theodore Dalrymple

About the author: *Theodore Dalrymple is a physician who treats patients in a British prison. He is a contributing editor to the quarterly* City Journal *and a columnist for the* Spectator, *a British weekly magazine.*

There is a progression in the minds of men: first the unthinkable becomes thinkable, and then it becomes an orthodoxy whose truth seems so obvious that no one remembers that anyone ever thought differently. This is just what is happening with the idea of legalizing drugs: it has reached the stage when millions of thinking men are agreed that allowing people to take whatever they like is the obvious, indeed only, solution to the social problems that arise from the consumption of drugs.

Intoxication and Restraint

Man's desire to take mind-altering substances is as old as society itself—as are attempts to regulate their consumption. If intoxication in one form or another is inevitable, then so is customary or legal restraint upon that intoxication. But no society until our own has had to contend with the ready availability of so many different mind-altering drugs, combined with a citizenry jealous of its right to pursue its own pleasures in its own way.

The arguments in favor of legalizing the use of all narcotic and stimulant drugs are twofold: philosophical and pragmatic. Neither argument is negligible, but both are mistaken, I believe, and both miss the point.

The Philosophic Argument

The philosophic argument is that, in a free society, adults should be permitted to do whatever they please, always provided that they are prepared to take the consequences of their own choices and that they cause no direct harm to others. The locus classicus for this point of view is John Stuart Mill's famous essay *On Liberty:* "The only purpose for which power can be rightfully exercised over

From Theodore Dalrymple, "Don't Legalize Drugs," *City Journal*, Spring 1997. Reprinted with permission.

any member of the community, against his will, is to prevent harm to others," Mill wrote. "His own good, either physical or moral, is not a sufficient warrant." This radical individualism allows society no part whatever in shaping, determining, or enforcing a moral code: in short, we have nothing in common but our contractual agreement not to interfere with one another as we go about seeking our private pleasures.

In practice, of course, it is exceedingly difficult to make people take *all* the consequences of their own actions—as they must, if Mill's great

> *"If intoxication in one form or another is inevitable, then so is customary or legal restraint upon that intoxication."*

principle is to serve as a philosophical guide to policy. Addiction to, or regular use of, most currently prohibited drugs cannot affect only the person who takes them—and not his spouse, children, neighbors, or employers. No man, except possibly a hermit, is an island; and so it is virtually impossible for Mill's principle to apply to any human action whatever, let alone shooting up heroin or smoking crack. Such a principle is virtually useless in determining what should or should not be permitted.

Perhaps we ought not be too harsh on Mill's principle: it's not clear that anyone has ever thought of a better one. But that is precisely the point. Human affairs cannot be decided by an appeal to an infallible rule, expressible in a few words, whose simple application can decide all cases, including whether drugs should be freely available to the entire adult population. Philosophical fundamentalism is not preferable to the religious variety; and because the desiderata of human life are many, and often in conflict with one another, mere philosophical inconsistency in policy—such as permitting the consumption of alcohol while outlawing cocaine—is not a sufficient argument against that policy. We all value freedom, and we all value order; sometimes we sacrifice freedom for order, and sometimes order for freedom. But once a prohibition has been removed, it is hard to restore, even when the newfound freedom proves to have been ill-conceived and socially disastrous.

Even Mill came to see the limitations of his own principle as a guide for policy and to deny that all pleasures were of equal significance for human existence. It was better, he said, to be Socrates discontented than a fool satisfied. Mill acknowledged that some goals were intrinsically worthier of pursuit than others.

Accepting Limitations

This being the case, not all freedoms are equal, and neither are all limitations of freedom: some are serious and some trivial. The freedom we cherish—or should cherish—is not merely that of satisfying our appetites, whatever they happen to be. We are not Dickensian Harold Skimpoles, exclaiming in protest that "Even the butterflies are free!" We are not children who chafe at restrictions *because* they are restrictions. And we even recognize the apparent paradox that some limitations to our freedoms have the consequence of making us freer overall. The freest man is not the one who slavishly follows his appetites and desires throughout his life—as all too many of my patients have discovered to their cost.

We are prepared to accept limitations to our freedoms for many reasons, not just that of public order. Take an extreme hypothetical case: public exhibitions of necrophilia are quite rightly not permitted, though on Mill's principle they should be. A corpse has no interests and cannot be harmed, because it is no longer a person; and no member of the public is harmed if he has agreed to attend such an exhibition.

Our resolve to prohibit such exhibitions would not be altered if we discovered that millions of people wished to attend them or even if we discovered that millions already were attending them illicitly. Our objection is not based upon pragmatic considerations or upon a head count: it is based upon the wrongness of the would-be exhibitions themselves. The fact that the prohibition represents a genuine restriction of our freedom is of no account.

Harmful Effects of Drugs

It might be argued that the freedom to choose among a variety of intoxicating substances is a much more important freedom and that millions of people have derived innocent fun from taking stimulants and narcotics. But the consumption of drugs has the effect of reducing men's freedom by circumscribing the range of their interests. It impairs their ability to pursue more important human aims, such as raising a family and fulfilling civic obligations. Very often it impairs their ability to pursue gainful employment and promotes parasitism. Moreover, far from being expanders of consciousness, most drugs severely limit it. One of the most striking characteristics of drug takers is their intense and tedious self-absorption; and their journeys into inner space are generally forays into inner vacuums. Drug taking is a lazy man's way of pursuing happiness and wisdom, and the shortcut turns out to be the deadest of dead ends. We lose remarkably little by not being permitted to take drugs.

"The consumption of drugs has the effect of reducing men's freedom by circumscribing the range of their interests."

The idea that freedom is merely the ability to act upon one's whims is surely very thin and hardly begins to capture the complexities of human existence; a man whose appetite is his law strikes us not as liberated but enslaved. And when such a narrowly conceived freedom is made the touchstone of public policy, a dissolution of society is bound to follow. No culture that makes publicly sanctioned self-indulgence its highest good can long survive: a radical egotism is bound to ensue, in which any limitations upon personal behavior are experienced as infringements of basic rights. Distinctions between the important and the trivial, between the freedom to criticize received ideas and the freedom to take LSD, are precisely the standards that keep societies from barbarism.

The Pragmatic Argument

So the legalization of drugs cannot be supported by philosophical principle. But if the pragmatic argument in favor of legalization were strong enough, it might overwhelm other objections. It is upon this argument that proponents of legalization rest the larger part of their case.

The argument is that the overwhelming majority of the harm done to society by the consumption of currently illicit drugs is caused not by their pharmacological properties but by their prohibition and the resultant criminal activity that prohibition always calls into being. Simple reflection tells us that a supply invariably grows up to meet a demand; and when the demand is widespread, suppression is useless. Indeed, it is harmful, since—by raising the price of the commodity in question—it raises the profits of middlemen, which gives them an even more powerful incentive to stimulate demand further. The vast profits to be made from cocaine and heroin—which, were it not for their illegality, would be cheap and easily affordable even by the poorest in affluent societies—exert a deeply corrupting effect on producers, distributors, consumers, and law enforcers alike. Besides, it is well known that illegality in itself has attractions for youth already inclined to disaffection. Even many of the harmful physical effects of illicit drugs stem from their illegal status: for example, fluctuations in the purity of heroin bought on the street are responsible for many of the deaths by overdose. If the sale and consumption of such drugs were legalized, consumers would know how much they were taking and thus avoid overdoses.

> *"If drugs were legalized, I suspect that the golden tree of life might spring some unpleasant surprises."*

Moreover, since society already permits the use of some mind-altering substances known to be both addictive and harmful, such as alcohol and nicotine, in prohibiting others it appears hypocritical, arbitrary, and dictatorial. Its hypocrisy, as well as its patent failure to enforce its prohibitions successfully, leads inevitably to a decline in respect for the law as a whole. Thus things fall apart, and the center cannot hold.

Problems Resolved?

It stands to reason, therefore, that all these problems would be resolved at a stroke if everyone were permitted to smoke, swallow, or inject anything he chose. The corruption of the police, the luring of children of 11 and 12 into illegal activities, the making of such vast sums of money by drug dealing that legitimate work seems pointless and silly by comparison, and the turf wars that make poor neighborhoods so exceedingly violent and dangerous, would all cease at once were drug taking to be decriminalized and the supply regulated in the same way as alcohol.

But a certain modesty in the face of an inherently unknowable future is surely advisable. That is why prudence is a political virtue: what stands to reason *should* happen does not necessarily happen in practice. As [German writer] Johann Wolfgang von Goethe said, all theory (even of the monetarist or free-market variety) is gray, but green springs the golden tree of life. If drugs were legalized, I suspect that the golden tree of life might spring some unpleasant surprises.

It is of course true, but only trivially so, that the present illegality of drugs is the cause of the criminality surrounding their distribution. Likewise, it is the illegality of stealing cars that creates car thieves. In fact, the ultimate cause of all criminality is law. As far as I am aware, no one has ever suggested that law should therefore be abandoned. Moreover, the impossibility of winning the "war" against theft, burglary, robbery, and fraud has never been used as an argument that these categories of crime should be abandoned. And so long as the demand for material goods outstrips supply, people will be tempted to commit criminal acts against the owners of property. This is not an argument, in my view, against private property or in favor of the common ownership of all goods. It does suggest, however, that we shall need a police force for a long time to come.

Reasons for Doubt

In any case, there are reasons to doubt whether the crime rate would fall quite as dramatically as advocates of legalization have suggested. Amsterdam, where access to drugs is relatively unproblematic, is among the most violent and squalid cities in Europe. The idea behind crime—of getting rich, or at least richer, quickly and without much effort—is unlikely to disappear once drugs are freely available to all who want them. And it may be that officially sanctioned antisocial behavior—the official lifting of taboos—breeds yet more antisocial behavior, as the "broken windows" theory would suggest.

Having met large numbers of drug dealers in prison, I doubt that they would return to respectable life if the principal article of their commerce were to be legalized. Far from evincing a desire to be reincorporated into the world of regular work, they express a deep contempt for it and regard those who accept the bargain of a fair day's work for a fair day's pay as cowards and fools. A life of crime has its attractions for many who would otherwise lead a mundane existence. So

> *"Opiate addicts who receive their drugs legally and free of charge continue to commit large numbers of crimes."*

long as there is the possibility of a lucrative racket or illegal traffic, such people will find it and extend its scope. Therefore, since even legalizers would hesitate to allow children to take drugs, decriminalization might easily result in dealers turning their attentions to younger and younger children, who—in the permissive atmosphere that even now prevails—have already been inducted into the drug subculture in alarmingly high numbers.

Reduction in Convictions

Those who do not deal in drugs but commit crimes to fund their consumption of them are, of course, more numerous than large-scale dealers. And it is true that once opiate addicts, for example, enter a treatment program, which often includes maintenance doses of methadone, the rate at which they commit crimes falls markedly. The drug clinic in my hospital claims an 80 percent reduction in criminal convictions among heroin addicts once they have been stabilized on methadone.

This is impressive, but it is not certain that the results should be generalized. First, the patients are self-selected: they have some motivation to change, otherwise they would not have attended the clinic in the first place. Only a minority of addicts attend, and therefore it is not safe to

> *"The demand for drugs, including opiates, would rise dramatically were their price to fall and their availability to increase."*

conclude that, if other addicts were to receive methadone, their criminal activity would similarly diminish.

Second, a decline in convictions is not necessarily the same as a decline in criminal acts. If methadone stabilizes an addict's life, he may become a more efficient, harder-to-catch criminal. Moreover, when the police in our city do catch an addict, they are less likely to prosecute him if he can prove that he is undergoing anything remotely resembling psychiatric treatment. They return him directly to his doctor. Having once had a psychiatric consultation is an all-purpose alibi for a robber or a burglar; the police, who do not want to fill in the 40-plus forms it now takes to charge anyone with anything in England, consider a single contact with a psychiatrist sufficient to deprive anyone of legal responsibility for crime forever.

Crime Remains High

Third, the rate of criminal activity among those drug addicts who receive methadone from the clinic, though reduced, remains very high. The deputy director of the clinic estimates that the number of criminal acts committed by his average patient (as judged by self-report) was 250 per year before entering treatment and 50 afterward. It may well be that the real difference is considerably less than this, because the patients have an incentive to exaggerate it to secure the continuation of their methadone. But clearly, opiate addicts who receive their drugs legally and free of charge continue to commit large numbers of crimes. In my clinics in prison, I see numerous prisoners who were on methadone when they committed the crime for which they are incarcerated.

Why do addicts given their drug free of charge continue to commit crimes? Some addicts, of course, continue to take drugs other than those prescribed and have to fund their consumption of them. So long as any restriction whatever regulates the consumption of drugs, many addicts will seek them illicitly, regardless of what they receive legally. In addition, the drugs themselves exert a long-term effect on a person's ability to earn a living and severely limit rather than expand his horizons and mental repertoire. They sap the will or the ability of an addict to make long-term plans. While drugs are the focus of an addict's life, they are not all he needs to live, and many addicts thus continue to procure the rest of what they need by criminal means.

Price and Availability

For the proposed legalization of drugs to have its much vaunted beneficial effect on the rate of criminality, such drugs would have to be both cheap and readily available. The legalizers assume that there is a natural limit to the demand for these drugs, and that if their consumption were legalized, the demand would not increase substantially. Those psychologically unstable persons currently taking drugs would continue to do so, with the necessity to commit crimes removed, while psychologically stabler people (such as you and I and our children) would not be enticed to take drugs by their new legal status and cheapness. But price and availability, I need hardly say, exert a profound effect on consumption: the cheaper alcohol becomes, for example, the more of it is consumed, at least within quite wide limits.

I have personal experience of this effect. I once worked as a doctor on a British government aid project to Africa. We were building a road through remote African bush. The contract stipulated that the construction company could import, free of all taxes, alcoholic drinks from the United Kingdom. These drinks the company then sold to its British workers at cost, in the local currency at the official exchange rate, which was approximately one-sixth the black-market rate. A liter bottle of gin thus cost less than a dollar and could be sold on the open market for almost ten dollars. So it was theoretically possible to remain dead drunk for several years for an initial outlay of less than a dollar.

Of course, the necessity to go to work somewhat limited the workers' consumption of alcohol. Nevertheless, drunkenness among them far

> *"The legal and liberal provision of drugs for people who are already addicted to them will not reduce the economic benefits to dealers of pushing these drugs."*

outstripped anything I have ever seen, before or since. I discovered that, when alcohol is effectively free of charge, a fifth of British construction workers will regularly go to bed so drunk that they are incontinent both of urine and feces. I remember one man who very rarely got as far as his bed at night: he fell asleep in the lavatory, where he was usually found the next morning. Half the men shook in the mornings and resorted to the hair of the dog to steady their hands before they drove their bulldozers and other heavy machines (which they frequently wrecked, at enormous expense to the British taxpayer); hangovers were universal. The men were either drunk or hung over for months on end.

Low Prices, Heavy Consumption

Sure, construction workers are notoriously liable to drink heavily, but in these circumstances even formerly moderate drinkers turned alcoholic and eventually suffered from delirium tremens. The heavy drinking occurred not because of the isolation of the African bush: not only did the company provide sports facilities for its workers, but there were many other ways to occupy oneself there. Other groups of workers in the bush whom I visited, who did not have the same rights of importation of alcoholic drink but had to purchase it at normal prices, were not nearly as drunk. And when the company asked its workers what it could do to improve their conditions, they unanimously asked for a further reduction in the price of alcohol, because they could think of nothing else to ask for.

> *"Once the use of a stimulant becomes culturally acceptable and normal, it can easily become so general as to exert devastating social effects."*

The conclusion was inescapable: that a susceptible population had responded to the low price of alcohol, and the lack of other effective restraints upon its consumption, by drinking destructively large quantities of it. The health of many men suffered as a consequence, as did their capacity for work; and they gained a well-deserved local reputation for reprehensible, violent, antisocial behavior.

It is therefore perfectly possible that the demand for drugs, including opiates, would rise dramatically were their price to fall and their availability to increase. And if it is true that the consumption of these drugs in itself predisposes to criminal behavior (as data from our clinic suggest), it is also possible that the effect on the rate of criminality of this rise in consumption would swamp the decrease that resulted from decriminalization. We would have just as much crime in aggregate as before, but many more addicts.

Britain's Opiate Problem

The intermediate position on drug legalization, such as that espoused by Ethan Nadelmann, director of the Lindesmith Center, a drug policy research institute sponsored by financier George Soros, is emphatically not the answer to drug-related crime. This view holds that it should be easy for addicts to receive opiate drugs from doctors, either free or at cost, and that they should receive them in municipal injecting rooms, such as now exist in Zurich. But just look at Liverpool, where 2,000 people of a population of 600,000 receive official prescriptions for methadone: this once proud and prosperous city is still the world capital of drug-motivated burglary, according to the police and independent researchers.

Of course, many addicts in Liverpool are not yet on methadone, because the clinics are insufficient in number to deal with the demand. If the city expended more money on clinics, perhaps the number of addicts in treatment could be increased five- or tenfold. But would that solve the problem of burglary in Liverpool? No, because the profits to be made from selling illicit opiates would still be large: dealers would therefore make efforts to expand into parts of the population hitherto relatively untouched, in order to protect their profits. The new addicts would still burgle to feed their habits. Yet more clinics dispensing yet more methadone would then be needed. In fact Britain, which has had a relatively liberal approach to the prescribing of opiate drugs to addicts since 1928 (I myself have prescribed heroin to addicts), has seen an explosive increase in addiction to opiates and all the evils associated with it since the 1960s, despite that liberal policy. A few hundred have become more than a hundred thousand.

At the heart of Nadelmann's position, then, is an evasion. The legal and liberal provision of drugs for people who are already addicted to them will not reduce the economic benefits to dealers of pushing these drugs, at least until the entire susceptible population is addicted and in a treatment program. So long as there are addicts who have to resort to the black market for their drugs, there will be drug-associated crime. Nadelmann assumes that the number of potential addicts wouldn't soar under considerably more liberal drug laws. I can't muster such Panglossian optimism.

The problem of reducing the amount of crime committed by individual addicts is emphatically not the same as the problem of reducing the amount of crime committed by addicts as a whole. I can illustrate what I mean by an analogy: it is often claimed that prison does not work because many prisoners are recidivists who, by definition, failed to be deterred from further wrongdoing by their last prison sentence. But does any sensible person believe that the abolition of prisons in their entirety would not reduce the numbers of the law-abiding? The murder rate in New York and the rate of drunken

> "We have already slid down enough slippery slopes in the last 30 years without looking for more such slopes to slide down."

driving in Britain have not been reduced by a sudden upsurge in the love of humanity, but by the effective threat of punishment. An institution such as prison can work for society even if it does not work for an individual.

Stimulant Drugs

The situation could be very much worse than I have suggested hitherto, however, if we legalized the consumption of drugs other than opiates. So far, I have considered only opiates, which exert a generally tranquilizing effect. If opiate addicts commit crimes even when they receive their drugs free of charge, it is because they are unable to meet their other needs any other way; but there are, unfortunately, drugs whose consumption directly leads to violence because of their psychopharmacological properties and not merely because of the criminality associated with their distribution. Stimulant drugs such as crack cocaine provoke paranoia, increase aggression, and promote violence. Much of this violence takes place in the home, as the relatives of crack takers will testify. It is something I know from personal acquaintance by working in the emergency room and in the wards of our hospital. Only someone who has not been assaulted by drug takers rendered psychotic by their drug could view with equanimity the prospect of the further spread of the abuse of stimulants.

And no one should underestimate the possibility that the use of stimulant drugs could spread very much wider, and become far more general, than it is now, if restraints on their use were relaxed. The importation of the mildly stimulant khat is legal in Britain, and a large proportion of the community of Somali refugees there devotes its entire life to chewing the leaves that contain the stimulant, miring these refugees in far worse poverty than they would otherwise experience. The reason that the khat habit has not spread to the rest of the population is that it takes an entire day's chewing of disgustingly bitter leaves to gain the comparatively mild pharmacological effect. The point is, however, that once the use of a stimulant becomes culturally acceptable and normal, it can easily become so general as to exert devastating social effects. And the kinds of stimulants on offer in Western cities—cocaine, crack, amphetamines—are vastly more attractive than khat.

The Wrong Question

In claiming that prohibition, not the drugs themselves, is the problem, Nadelmann and many others—even policemen—have said that "the war on drugs is lost." But to demand a yes or no answer to the question "Is the war against drugs being won?" is like demanding a yes or no answer to the question "Have you stopped beating your wife yet?" Never can an unimaginative and fundamentally stupid metaphor have exerted a more baleful effect upon proper thought.

Let us ask whether medicine is winning the war against death. The answer is obviously no, it isn't winning: the one fundamental rule of human existence remains, unfortunately, one man one death. And this is despite the fact that 14 percent of the gross domestic product of the United States (to say nothing of the efforts of other countries) goes into the fight against death. Was ever a war more expensively lost? Let us then abolish medical schools, hospitals, and departments of public health. If every man has to die, it doesn't matter very much when he does so.

If the war against drugs is lost, then so are the wars against theft, speeding, incest, fraud, rape, murder, arson, and illegal parking. Few, if any, such wars are winnable. So let us all do anything we choose.

Even the legalizers' argument that permitting the purchase and use of drugs as freely as Milton Friedman suggests will necessarily result in less governmental and other official interference in our lives doesn't stand up. To the contrary, if the use of narcotics and stimulants were to become virtually universal, as is by no means impossible, the number of situations in which compulsory checks upon people would have to be carried out, for reasons of public safety, would increase enormously. Pharmacies, banks, schools, hospitals—indeed, all organizations dealing with the public—might feel obliged to check regularly and randomly on the drug consumption of their employees. The general use of such drugs would increase the *locus standi* [standing place] of innumerable agencies, public and private, to interfere in our lives; and freedom from interference, far from having increased, would have drastically shrunk.

Cause for Skepticism

The present situation is bad, undoubtedly; but few are the situations so bad that they cannot be made worse by a wrong policy decision. The extreme intellectual elegance of the proposal to legalize the distribution and consumption of drugs, touted as the solution to so many problems at once (AIDS, crime, overcrowding in the prisons, and even the attractiveness of drugs to foolish young people) should give rise to skepticism. Social problems are not usually like that. Analogies with the Prohibition era, often drawn by those who would legalize drugs, are false and inexact: it is one thing to attempt to ban a substance that has been in customary use for centuries by at least nine-tenths of the adult population, and quite another to retain a ban on substances that are still not in customary use, in an attempt to ensure that they never do become customary. Surely we have already slid down enough slippery slopes in the last 30 years without looking for more such slopes to slide down.

Legalizing Drugs Would Increase Violent Crime

by James A. Inciardi and Christine A. Saum

About the authors: *James A. Inciardi is the director of, and Christine A. Saum is a research associate at, the Center for Drug and Alcohol Studies at the University of Delaware in Newark.*

Frustrated by the government's apparent inability to reduce the supply of illegal drugs on the streets of America, and disquieted by media accounts of innocents victimized by drug-related violence, some policy makers are convinced that the "war on drugs" has failed. In an attempt to find a better solution to the "drug crisis" or, at the very least, to try an alternative strategy, they have proposed legalizing drugs.

Arguments from Both Sides

They argue that, if marijuana, cocaine, heroin, and other drugs were legalized, several positive things would probably occur: (1) drug prices would fall; (2) users would obtain their drugs at low, government-regulated prices, and they would no longer be forced to resort to crime in order to support their habits; (3) levels of drug-related crime, and particularly violent crime, would significantly decline, resulting in less crowded courts, jails, and prisons (this would allow law-enforcement personnel to focus their energies on the "real criminals" in society); and (4) drug production, distribution, and sale would no longer be controlled by organized crime, and thus such criminal syndicates as the Colombian cocaine "cartels," the Jamaican "posses," and the various "mafias" around the country and the world would be decapitalized, and the violence associated with drug distribution rivalries would be eliminated.

By contrast, the anti-legalization camp argues that violent crime would not necessarily decline in a legalized drug market. In fact, there are three reasons why it might actually increase. First, removing the criminal sanctions against the possession and distribution of illegal drugs would make them more available and attractive and, hence, would create large numbers of new users. Sec-

From James A. Inciardi and Christine A. Saum, "Legalization Madness." Reprinted with permission of the authors and the *Public Interest*, no. 123, Spring 1996, pp. 72–82; ©1996 by National Affairs Inc.

ond, an increase in use would lead to a greater number of dysfunctional addicts who could not support themselves, their habits, or their lifestyles through legitimate means. Hence crime would be their only alternative. Third, more users would mean more of the violence associated with the ingestion of drugs.

These divergent points of view tend to persist because the relationships between drugs and crime are quite complex and because the possible outcomes of a legalized drug market are based primarily on speculation.

> *"Removing the criminal sanctions against the possession and distribution of illegal drugs would . . . create large numbers of new users."*

However, it is possible, from a careful review of the existing empirical literature on drugs and violence, to make some educated inferences.

Considering "Legalization"

Yet much depends upon what we mean by "legalizing drugs." Would all currently illicit drugs be legalized or would the experiment be limited to just certain ones? True legalization would be akin to selling such drugs as heroin and cocaine on the open market, much like alcohol and tobacco, with a few age-related restrictions. In contrast, there are "medicalization" and "decriminalization" alternatives. Medicalization approaches are of many types, but, in essence, they would allow users to obtain prescriptions for some, or all, currently illegal substances. Decriminalization removes the criminal penalties associated with the possession of small amounts of illegal drugs for personal use, while leaving intact the sanctions for trafficking, distribution, and sale.

But what about crack-cocaine? A quick review of the literature reveals that the legalizers, the decriminalizers, and the medicalizers avoid talking about this particular form of cocaine. Perhaps they do not want to legalize crack out of fear of the drug itself, or of public outrage. Arnold S. Trebach, a professor of law at American University and president of the Drug Policy Foundation, is one of the very few who argues for the full legalization of all drugs, including crack. He explains, however, that most are reluctant to discuss the legalization of crack-cocaine because, "it is a very dangerous drug. . . . I know that for many people the very thought of making crack legal destroys any inclination they might have had for even thinking about drug-law reform."

There is a related concern associated with the legalization of cocaine. Because crack is easily manufactured from powder cocaine (just add water and baking soda and cook on a stove or in a microwave), many drug-policy reformers hold that no form of cocaine should be legalized. But this weakens the argument that legalization will reduce drug-related violence; for much of this violence would appear to be in the cocaine- and crack-distribution markets.

To better understand the complex relationship between drugs and violence, we will discuss the data in the context of three models developed by Paul J. Goldstein of the University of Illinois at Chicago. They are the "psychopharmacological," "economically compulsive," and "systemic" explanations of violence. The first model holds, correctly in our view, that some individuals may become excitable, irrational, and even violent due to the ingestion of specific drugs. In contrast, taking a more economic approach to the behavior of drug users, the second holds that some drug users engage in violent crime mainly for the sake of supporting their drug use. The third model maintains that drug-related violent crime is simply the result of the drug market under a regime of illegality.

Psychopharmacological Violence

The case for legalization rests in part upon the faulty assumption that drugs themselves do not cause violence; rather, so goes the argument, violence is the result of depriving drug addicts of drugs or of the "criminal" trafficking in drugs. But, as researcher Barry Spunt points out, "Users of drugs do get violent when they get high."

Research has documented that chronic users of amphetamines, methamphetamine, and cocaine in particular tend to exhibit hostile and aggressive behaviors. Psychopharmacological violence can also be a product of what is known as "cocaine psychosis." As dose and duration of cocaine use increase, the development of cocaine-related psychopathology is not uncommon. Cocaine psychosis is generally preceded by a transitional period characterized by increased suspiciousness, compulsive behavior, fault finding, and even-

> *"The case for legalization rests in part upon the faulty assumption that drugs themselves do not cause violence."*

tually paranoia. When the psychotic state is reached, individuals may experience visual, as well as auditory, hallucinations, with persecutory voices commonly heard. Many believe that they are being followed by police or that family, friends, and others are plotting against them.

Moreover, everyday events are sometimes misinterpreted by cocaine users in ways that support delusional beliefs. When coupled with the irritability and hyperactivity that cocaine tends to generate in almost all of its users, the cocaine-induced paranoia may lead to violent behavior as a means of "self-defense" against imagined persecutors. The violence associated with cocaine psychosis is a common feature in many crack houses across the United States. Violence may also result from the irritability associated with drug-withdrawal syndromes. In addition, some users ingest drugs before committing crimes to both loosen inhibitions and bolster their resolve to break the law.

Acts of violence may result from either periodic or chronic use of a drug. For example, in a study of drug use and psychopathy among Baltimore City jail inmates, researchers at the University of Baltimore reported that cocaine use was related to irritability, resentment, hostility, and assault. They concluded that these indicators of aggression may be a function of drug effects rather than of a predisposition to these behaviors. Similarly, Barry Spunt and his colleagues at National Development and Research Institutes (NDRI) in New York City found that of 269 convicted murderers incarcerated in New York State prisons, 45 percent were high at the time of the offense. Three in 10 believed that the homicide was related to their drug use, challenging conventional beliefs that violence only infrequently occurs as a result of drug consumption.

> *"Even marijuana, which pro-legalizers consider harmless, may have a connection with violence and crime."*

Even marijuana, which pro-legalizers consider harmless, may have a connection with violence and crime. Spunt and his colleagues attempted to determine the role of marijuana in the crimes of the homicide offenders they interviewed in the New York State prisons. One-third of those who had ever used marijuana had smoked the drug in the 24-hour period prior to the homicide. Moreover, 31 percent of those who considered themselves to be "high" at the time of committing murder felt that the homicide and marijuana were related. William Blount of the University of South Florida interviewed abused women in prisons and shelters for battered women located throughout Florida. He and his colleagues found that 24 percent of those who killed their abusers were marijuana users while only 8 percent of those who did not kill their abusers smoked marijuana.

Alcohol Abuse

A point that needs emphasizing is that alcohol, because it is legal, accessible, and inexpensive, is linked to violence to a far greater extent than any illegal drug. For example, in the study just cited, it was found that an impressive 64 percent of those women who eventually killed their abusers were alcohol users (44 percent of those who did not kill their abusers were alcohol users). Indeed, the extent to which alcohol is responsible for violent crimes in comparison with other drugs is apparent from the statistics. For example, Carolyn Block and her colleagues at the Criminal Justice Information Authority in Chicago found that, between 1982 and 1989, the use of alcohol by offenders or victims in local homicides ranged from 18 percent to 32 percent.

Alcohol has, in fact, been consistently linked to homicide. Spunt and his colleagues interviewed 268 homicide offenders incarcerated in New York State correctional facilities to determine the role of alcohol in their crimes: Thirty-one percent of the respondents reported being drunk at the time of the crime and 19 percent believed that the homicide was related to their drinking. More generally, Douglass Murdoch of Quebec's McGill University found that in some 9,000 criminal cases drawn from a multinational sample, 62 percent of violent offenders were drinking shortly before, or at the time of, the offense.

It appears that alcohol reduces the inhibitory control of threat, making it more likely that a person will exhibit violent behaviors normally suppressed by fear. In turn, this reduction of inhibition heightens the probability that intoxicated persons will perpetrate, or become victims of, aggressive behavior.

When analyzing the psychopharmacological model of drugs and violence, most of the discussions focus on the offender and the role of drugs in causing or facilitating crime. But what about the victims? Are the victims of drug- and alcohol-related homicides simply casualties of someone else's substance abuse? In addressing these questions, the data demonstrates that victims are likely to be drug users as well. For example, in an analysis of the 4,298 homicides that occurred in New York City during 1990 and 1991, Kenneth Tardiff of Cornell University Medical College found that the victims of these offenses were 10 to 50 times more likely to be cocaine users than were members of the general population. Of the white female victims, 60 percent in the 25- to 34-year age group had cocaine in their systems; for black females, the figure was 72 percent. Tardiff speculated

> *"A great many of the victims of homicide and other forms of violence are drinkers and drug users themselves."*

that the classic symptoms of cocaine use—irritability, paranoia, aggressiveness—may have instigated the violence. In another study of cocaine users in New York City, female high-volume users were found to be victims of violence far more frequently than low-volume and nonusers of cocaine. Studies in numerous other cities and countries have yielded the same general findings—that a great many of the victims of homicide and other forms of violence are drinkers and drug users themselves.

Economically Compulsive Violence

Supporters of the economically compulsive model of violence argue that in a legalized market, the prices of "expensive drugs" would decline to more affordable levels, and, hence, predatory crimes would become unnecessary. This argument is based on several specious assumptions. First, it assumes that there is empirical support for what has been referred to as the "enslavement theory of addiction." Second, it assumes that people addicted to drugs commit crimes only for the purpose of supporting their habits. Third, it assumes that, in a legalized market, users could obtain as much of the drugs as they wanted whenever they wanted. Finally, it assumes that, if drugs are inexpensive, they will be affordable, and thus crime would be unnecessary.

With respect to the first premise, there has been for the better part of the twentieth century a concerted belief among many in the drug-policy field that addicts commit crimes because they are "enslaved" to drugs, and further that, because of the high price of heroin, cocaine, and other illicit chemicals on the black market, users are forced to commit crimes in order to support their drug habits. However, there is no solid empirical evidence to support this contention.

From the 1920s through the end of the 1960s, hundreds of studies of the relationship between crime and addiction were conducted. Invariably, when one analysis would support the posture of "enslavement theory," the next would affirm the view that addicts were criminals first and that their drug use was but one more manifestation of their deviant lifestyles. In retrospect, the difficulty lay in the ways that many of the studies had been conducted: Biases and deficiencies in research designs and sampling had rendered their findings of little value.

"Addicts commit crimes for reasons other than supporting their drug habit. They do so also for daily living expenses."

Studies since the mid 1970s of active drug users on the streets of New York, Miami, Baltimore, and elsewhere have demonstrated that the "enslavement theory" has little basis in reality. All of these studies of the criminal careers of drug users have convincingly documented that, while drug use tends to intensify and perpetuate criminal behavior, it usually does not initiate criminal careers. In fact, the evidence suggests that among the majority of street drug users who are involved in crime, their criminal careers are well established prior to the onset of either narcotics or cocaine use. As such, it would appear that the "inference of causality"—that the high price of drugs on the black market itself causes crime—is simply false.

Living Expenses

Looking at the second premise, a variety of studies show that addicts commit crimes for reasons other than supporting their drug habit. They do so also for daily living expenses. For example, researchers at the Center for Drug and Alcohol Studies at the University of Delaware who studied crack users on the streets of Miami found that, of the active addicts interviewed, 85 percent of the male and 70 percent of the female interviewees paid for portions of their living expenses through street crime. In fact, one-half of the men and one-fourth of the women paid for 90 percent or more of their living expenses through crime. And, not surprisingly, 96 percent of the men and 99 percent of the women had not held a legal job in the 90-day period before being interviewed for the study.

With respect to the third premise, that in a legalized market users could obtain as much of the drugs as they wanted whenever they wanted, only speculation is possible. More than likely, however, there would be some sort of regulation, and hence black markets for drugs would persist for those whose addictions were beyond the medicalized or legalized allotments. In a decriminalized market, levels of drug-related violence would likely either remain unchanged or increase (if drug use increased).

As for the last premise, that cheap drugs preclude the need to commit crimes to obtain them, the evidence emphatically suggests that this is not the case. Consider crack-cocaine: Although crack "rocks" are available on the illegal market for as little as two dollars in some locales, users are still involved in crime-driven endeavors to support their addictions. For example, researchers Norman S. Miller and Mark S. Gold surveyed 200 consecutive callers to the 1-800-COCAINE hotline who considered themselves to have a problem with crack. They found that, despite the low cost of crack, 63 percent of daily users and 40 percent of non-daily users spent more than $200 per week on the drug. Similarly, interviews conducted by NDRI researchers in New York City with almost 400 drug users contacted in the streets, jails, and treatment programs revealed that almost one-half of them spent over $1,000 a month on crack. The study also documented that crack users—despite the low cost of their drug of choice—spent more money on drugs than did users of heroin, powder cocaine, marijuana, and alcohol.

Systemic Violence

It is the supposed systemic violence associated with trafficking in cocaine and crack in America's inner cities that has recently received the attention of drug-policy critics interested in legalizing drugs. Certainly it might appear that, if heroin and cocaine were legal substances, systemic drug-related violence would decline. However, there are two very important questions in this regard: First, is drug-related violence more often psychopharmacological or systemic? Second, is the great bulk of systemic violence related to the distribution of crack? If most of the drug-related violence is psychopharmacological in nature, and if systemic violence is typically related to crack—the drug generally excluded from consideration when legalization is recommended—then legalizing drugs would probably *not* reduce violent crime.

Regarding the first question, several studies conducted in New York City tend to contradict, or at least not support, the notion that legalizing drugs would reduce violent, systemic-related crime. For example, Paul J. Goldstein's ethnographic studies of male and female drug users during the late 1980s found that cocaine-related violence was more often psychopharmacological than systemic.

> *"Legalizing drugs would probably **not** reduce violent crime."*

Similarly, Kenneth Tardiff's study of 4,298 New York City homicides found that 31 percent of the victims had used cocaine in the 24-hour period prior to their deaths. One of the conclusions of the study was that the homicides were not necessarily related to drug dealing. In all likelihood, as victims of homicide, the cocaine users may have provoked violence through their irritability, paranoid thinking, and verbal or physical aggression—all of which are among the psychopharmacological effects of cocaine.

Regarding the second question, the illegal drug most associated with systemic violence is crack-cocaine. Of all illicit drugs, crack is the one now responsible for the most homicides. In a study done in New York City in 1988 by Goldstein and his colleagues, crack was found to be connected with 32 percent of all homicides and 60 percent of all drug-related homicides. Furthermore, although there is evidence that crack sellers are more violent than other drug sellers, this violence is not confined to the drug-selling context—violence potentials appear to precede involvement in selling.

Thus, though crack has been blamed for increasing violence in the marketplace, this violence actually stems from the psychopharmacological consequences of crack use. Ansley Hamid, a professor of anthropology at the John Jay College of Criminal Justice in New York, reasons that increases in crack-related violence are due to the deterioration of informal and formal social controls throughout communities that have been destabilized by economic processes and political decisions. If this is the case, does anyone really believe that we can improve these complex social problems through the simple act of legalizing drugs?

> *"Legalizing drugs would likely increase physical illnesses and compound any existing psychiatric problems among users and their family members."*

Don't Just Say No

The issue of whether or not legalization would create a multitude of new users also needs to be addressed. It has been shown that many people do not use drugs simply because drugs are illegal. As Mark A.R. Kleiman, author of *Against Excess: Drug Policy for Results*, put it: "Illegality by itself tends to suppress consumption, independent of its effect on price, both because some consumers are reluctant to disobey the law and because illegal products are harder to find and less reliable as to quality and labeling than legal ones."

Although there is no way of accurately estimating how many new users there would be if drugs were legalized, there would probably be many. To begin with, there is the historical example of Prohibition. During Prohibition, there was a decrease of 20 percent to 50 percent in the number of alcoholics. These estimates were calculated based on a decline in cirrhosis and other alcohol-related deaths; after Prohibition ended, both of these indicators increased.

Currently, relatively few people are steady users of drugs. The University of Michigan's *Monitoring the Future* study reported in 1995 that only two-tenths of 1 percent of high-school seniors are daily users of either hallucinogens, cocaine, heroin, sedatives, or inhalants. It is the addicts who overwhelmingly consume the bulk of the drug supply—80 percent of all alcohol and almost 100 percent of all heroin. In other words, there are significantly large numbers of non-users who have yet to even try drugs, let alone use them regularly. Of those who begin to use drugs "recreationally," researchers estimate that approximately 10 percent go on to serious, heavy, chronic, compulsive use. Herbert Kleber, the former deputy director of the Office of National Drug Control Policy, recently estimated that cocaine legalization might multiply the number of addicts from the current 2 million to between 18 and 50 million (which are the estimated numbers of problem drinkers and nicotine addicts).

This suggests that drug prohibition seems to be having some very positive effects and that legalizing drugs would not necessarily have a depressant effect on violent crime. With legalization, violent crime would likely escalate; or perhaps some types of systemic violence would decline at the expense of greatly increasing the overall rate of violent crime. Moreover, legalizing drugs would likely increase physical illnesses and compound any existing psychiatric problems among users and their family members. And finally, legalizing drugs would not eliminate the effects of unemployment, inadequate housing, deficient job skills, economic worries, and physical abuse that typically contribute to the use of drugs.

Legalizing Drugs Would Increase Drug Use

by Mortimer B. Zuckerman

About the author: *Mortimer B. Zuckerman is the editor in chief of the weekly newsmagazine* U.S. News & World Report.

We are at a critical stage in the intermittent war on drugs. The plausible case for allowing sick patients access to marijuana for the relief of pain, approved by California and Arizona voters [in November 1996], has given impetus to those who would legalize drugs altogether. They are dangerously wrong. If marijuana is to be approved for hospital medicine, it is essential that general use be more rigorously curtailed. The narrow window of legitimacy in medicine will be a menace if it becomes a wide-open door.

The Legalizers' View

The argument of the legalizers is that America has lost the drug war. No matter how many fast boats, helicopters, and antinarcotics teams we have, illegal drug use continues and so does the criminal apparatus that supports the trade. If drugs were legalized at low prices the gangs and peddlers would be out of business and the killings and extortions would disappear. In a democracy, in short, it is a mistake to criminalize the behavior of so many people. It promotes crime and weakens respect for the rule of law.

There are many things amiss with this analysis. The drug war is not being lost. In 1979, some 25 million had tried drugs sometime in the preceding month. Today that figure is 11 million. Why? Because of stricter drug laws, stronger societal disapproval, and an increased awareness of the devastation drugs can produce.

Within the brighter general picture, there is an ominous trend. Drug use has increased threefold among young teens from 1992 to 1996. They think they are immune and can limit their involvement to soft drugs. That is a delusion—like trying to be a little bit pregnant. The earlier and more frequently an adolescent uses a soft drug the more likely it is he will go on to the hard drugs. This is surely an argument for more vigilance, not less. Legalization would jeopardize a whole generation.

Legalization Would Increase Access

The legalizers respond that if drugs were legal, it would not increase the number of addicts, since anyone who wants a drug can get it now. This does not square with the facts. Drugs are not accessible at all. According to research, fewer than 50 percent of high school seniors and young adults under 22 believed that they could obtain cocaine "fairly easily" or "very easily." Only 39 percent of the adult population reported that they could get cocaine. So, after legalization, you could double or triple the number of people who would have access to drugs and who would assuredly use them—exactly the history of alcohol when Prohibition ended.

An even more absurd legalization argument is that young people could be excluded from the free market for drugs. How could we do that when we have been unable to keep legal drugs—tobacco and alcohol—out of the hands of children? Five million children smoke and 12 million teens drink. Nor should we overlook that the stigma of illegality has been important in discouraging kids from experimenting. In separate studies, 60 percent to 70 percent of New Jersey and California students reported that "fear of getting in trouble with the authorities was a major reason why they did not use drugs." Another study found that "the greater the perceived likelihood of apprehension and swift punishment for using marijuana, the less likely adolescents are to smoke it."

A Dreadful Prospect

Imagine the prospect that the number of drug users would approach the number of alcohol abusers (more than 18 million) or tobacco addicts. One expert estimates that legalizing cocaine would increase the number of addicts 10-fold to about 20 million. If millions become addicted in a period when drugs are illegal, socially unacceptable, and generally difficult to get, then millions more will surely become addicts when drugs are legally and socially acceptable and easily obtainable.

We should always be suspicious of simple solutions to complex problems. Legalization is such a bromide. The National Center on Addiction

> *"Legalization would jeopardize a whole generation."*

and Substance Abuse at Columbia University had it right: "Drugs are not a threat to American society because they are illegal; they are illegal because they are a threat to American society." They should remain that way.

Arguments for Legalizing Drugs Are Specious

by Joseph A. Califano Jr.

About the author: *Joseph A. Califano Jr. is the president of the Center on Addiction and Substance Abuse at Columbia University in New York City and was the secretary of Health, Education, and Welfare in the Carter administration.*

When high priests of America's political right and left as articulate as William F. Buckley Jr., founding editor of *National Review*, and Anthony Lewis, a columnist for the *New York Times* Op-Ed page, peddle the same drug legalization line, it's time to shout caveat emptor—let the buyer beware. For the boomlet to legalize drugs like heroin, cocaine and marijuana that they—and magazines like *National Review* and *New York*—are trying to seed among the right and left ends of the political spectrum, is founded in fiction, not fact. And it's our children who could suffer long-lasting, permanent damage.

Fewer Drug Users

Fiction: There's been no progress in the war on drugs.

Fact: The U.S. Department of Health and Human Services' National Household Drug Survey, the nation's most extensive assessment of drug use, reports that from 1979 to 1994 the number of current drug users (those using within the past month) has dropped from 24.8 million to 13 million, marijuana users from 23 million to 10 million and cocaine users from 4.4 million to 1.4 million. The number of hard-core addicts has held steady at around 6 million, a situation most experts attribute to the unavailability of treatment and the large number of addicts in the pipeline.

Fiction: Whether to use drugs and become hooked is an adult decision.

Fact: It's children who choose. Hardly anyone in America begins drug use after age 21. An individual who does not smoke, use drugs or abuse alcohol by age 21 is virtually certain never to do so. The nicotine pushers understand this, which is why they fight so strenuously to kill efforts to keep their stuff away from kids.

From Joseph A. Califano Jr., "Fictions and Facts About Drug Legalization," *America*, March 16, 1996. Reprinted by permission of the author.

Fiction: Legalization would be only for adults; legalized drugs would not be available to children.

Fact: Nothing in the American experience gives grounds to believe in our ability to keep legal drugs out of the hands of children. It's illegal for children to purchase cigarettes and alcohol. But today, 3 million adolescents smoke an average of half a pack a day: a $1 billion a year market. Twelve million underage Americans drink: a $10 billion a year market.

Under the Influence

Fiction: Legalization would reduce crime and social problems.

Fact: Any short-term reduction in arrests from repealing drug laws would quickly evaporate as use increased; and the criminal conduct—assaults, murders, rapes, child molestations, vandalism and other violence—spawned by drugs like cocaine and methamphetamines would explode. The U.S. Department of Justice reports that criminals commit six times as many homicides, four times as many assaults and almost one and a half times as many robberies under the influence of drugs as they commit in order to get money to buy drugs.

Here the history of our experience with alcohol can teach us. More state prisoners were drunk on alcohol than high on drugs when they committed their crimes, and America's number one criminal offense is driving while intoxicated (1.5 million arrests in 1993). Health and welfare costs would skyrocket if drugs were legalized.

Fiction: The American experience with the prohibition of alcohol supports drug legalization.

Fact: This ignores two important distinctions: Prohibition was in fact decriminalization (possession of alcohol for personal consumption was not illegal); and alcohol, unlike illegal drugs such as heroin and cocaine, has a long history of broad social acceptance dating back to the Old Testament and Ancient Greece. Nevertheless, alcohol consumption dropped from 1.96 gallons per person in 1919 to 0.97 gallons per person in 1934, the first full year after Prohibition ended. Death rates from cirrhosis among men came down from 29.5 per 100,000 in 1911 to 10.7 per 100,000 in 1929. During Prohibition, admission to mental health institutions for alcohol psychosis dropped 60 percent; arrests for drunk and disorderly conduct went down 50 percent; welfare agencies reported significant declines in cases due to alcohol-related family problems, and the death rate from impure alcohol did not rise.

> *"Any short-term reduction in arrests from repealing drug laws would quickly evaporate as use increased."*

Nor did Prohibition generate a crime wave. Homicide increased at a higher rate between 1900 and 1910 than during Prohibition, and organized crime was well established in the cities before 1920. I put these facts on the record not to support a return to Prohibition, which I strongly oppose, but to set the historical record straight and temper the revisionist view of legalizers who take their history from celluloid images of 1930's gangster movies.

A Potential Disaster

Fiction: Greater availability and legal acceptability of drugs like marijuana, cocaine and heroin would not increase use.

Fact: This contradicts not only experience but human nature. In the 1970's we decriminalized marijuana. The Schafer Commission appointed by President Richard M. Nixon recommended decriminalization, as did President Jimmy Carter. The result? A soaring increase in marijuana use, particularly among youngsters.

Today we have 50 million nicotine addicts, 18 million alcoholics and alcohol abusers and 6 million illegal drug addicts. Experts like Dr. Herbert Kleber at Columbia University believe that with legalization the number of cocaine addicts alone would jump beyond the number of alcoholics.

> *"Experts ... believe that with legalization the number of cocaine addicts alone would jump beyond the number of alcoholics."*

That spells big trouble. In 1995 illegal drugs killed 20,000 Americans. Tobacco was responsible for 450,000 deaths; alcohol for more than 100,000. Studies at the Center on Addiction and Substance Abuse at Columbia University reveal that, of the $66 billion that substance abuse costs Federal health and disability entitlement programs like Medicare and Medicaid, $56 billion is attributable to tobacco and alcohol.

Affecting the Self and Others

Fiction: Drug use is an issue of civil liberties.

Fact: This is a convenient misreading of John Stuart Mill's *On Liberty*. Legalizers cite Mill to argue that the state has no right to interfere in the private life of a citizen who uses drugs; only when an action harms someone else may the state take action to prevent it. They ignore the fact that Mill's conception of freedom does not extend to the right of individuals to enslave themselves or to decide that they will give up their liberty. Mill wrote with blunt clarity: "The principle of freedom cannot require that he should be free not to be free. It is not freedom to be allowed to alienate his freedom."

Drug addiction is a form of enslavement. It "alters pathologically the nature and character of abusers," says Mitchell Rosenthal, M.D., the president of Phoenix House. Even Mill at his most expansive would admit that the state can take action not only to free an addict from chains of chemical dependency that take away the freedom to be all that God meant him or her to be, but also to prevent those bonds from becoming shackles in the first place. Indeed, a state devoted to individual freedom has an obligation to nourish a society and legal structure that protects individuals from the slavery of drug addiction.

Even Mill's most libertarian contention—that the state can regulate only those actions that directly affect others—does not support individual drug abuse and addiction, because such conduct does directly affect others: from the abused spouse and baby involuntarily addicted through the mother's umbilical cord, to co-workers and innocent bystanders injured or killed by adolescents high on crack cocaine. In a society as interdependent as ours, the drug abuser's conduct has a direct and substantial impact on every taxpayer who foots the bill for the criminal and health cost consequences of the drug abuser's actions.

Certainly a society that recognizes the state's compelling interest in banning (and stopping individuals from using) lead paint, asbestos insulation, unsafe toys and flammable fabrics can hardly ignore its interest in banning cocaine, heroin, marijuana, methamphetamines and hallucinogens. Indeed, refusing to include drug use in the right of privacy, the Supreme Court has blessed state laws that prohibit even the sacramental use of peyote. With the exception of Alaska, state courts, like those of New York, have held that possession of marijuana in the home is not protected by the right of privacy.

Failures in Europe

Fiction: Legalization works well in European countries.

Fact: The ventures of Switzerland, England and the Netherlands into drug legalization have had disastrous consequences. Switzerland's "Needle Park," touted as a way to restrict a few hundred heroin addicts to a small area, turned into a grotesque tourist attraction of 20,000 heroin addicts and junkies, which had to be closed down before it infected the city of Zurich. England's foray into allowing any doctor to prescribe heroin was quickly curbed as heroin use increased.

The Netherlands legalized marijuana for anyone over age 15. Adolescent pot use there rose nearly 200 percent while it was dropping 66 percent in the United States. As crime and the availability of drugs like heroin and cocaine rose, and

> *"The ventures of Switzerland, England and the Netherlands into drug legalization have had disastrous consequences."*

complaints from city residents about the decline in their quality of life multiplied, the Amsterdam city council moved to raise the age for legal purchase of marijuana from 16 to 18 and trim back the number of pot distribution shops in Amsterdam. Dutch persistence in selling pot has angered European neighbors because the Netherlands' wide-open attitude toward marijuana is believed to be spreading pot and other drugs beyond its borders. And Sweden, after a brief turn at permitting doctors to give drugs to addicts, in 1980 adopted the American policy of seeking a drug-free society. By 1988, Sweden had seen drug use among young Army conscripts drop 75 percent and current use by ninth graders fall 66 percent.

Chapter 4

What is most disturbing about the arguments for legalization is that they glide over the impact such a policy would have on our children. The United States is assuredly not the Garden of Eden of the Old Testament. Dealing with evil, including drugs, is part of the human experience. But there is a special obligation to protect our children from evil, and drugs are first and foremost an issue about our children. It is adolescent experimentation that leads to abuse and addiction.

Today, most kids don't use illicit drugs. But all children, particularly the poorest, are vulnerable to abuse and addiction. Russian roulette is not a game anyone should play. Legalizing drugs is not only playing Russian roulette with our children. It's slipping a couple of extra bullets in the chamber.

Bibliography

Books

Ronald Bayer, ed.	*Confronting Drug Policy: Illicit Drugs in a Free Society.* New York: Cambridge University Press, 1993.
William Bennett	*Body Count: Moral Poverty—and How to Win America's War Against Crime and Drugs.* New York: Simon & Schuster, 1996.
Rod L. Evans and Irwin M. Berent, eds.	*Drug Legalization: For and Against.* La Salle, IL:Open Court, 1992.
Dean R. Gerstein and Lawrence W. Green, eds.	*Preventing Drug Abuse: What Do We Know?* Washington, DC: National Academy Press, 1993.
Lester Grinspoon	*Marihuana Reconsidered: The Most Thorough Evaluation of the Benefits and Dangers of Cannabis.* Cambridge, MA: Harvard University Press, 1994.
Gail Mitchell Hoyt	*The Worker, the Firm, and the Decision to Use Drugs.* New York: Garland, 1995.
Howard T. Milhorn	*Drug and Alcohol Abuse: The Authoritative Guide for Parents, Teachers, and Counselors.* New York: Plenum, 1994.
Philip P. Muisener	*Understanding and Treating Adolescent Substance Abuse.* Thousand Oaks, CA: Sage, 1994.
Jacques Normand, Richard O. Lempert, and Charles P. O'Brien, eds.	*Under the Influence? Drugs and the American Work Force.* Washington, DC: National Research Council/Institute of Medicine, 1994.
Ann Marie Pagliaro and Louis A. Pagliaro	*Substance Use Among Children and Adolescents: Its Nature, Extent, and Effects from Conception to Adulthood.* New York: John Wiley, 1996.
David A. Peters	*The Probability of Addiction: Legal, Medical, and Social Implications.* San Francisco: Austin & Winfield, 1997.
Paul B. Stares	*Global Habit: The Drug Problem in a Borderless World.* Washington, DC: Brookings Institution, 1996.

Bibliography

Periodicals

William F. Buckley Jr., ed.	"400 Readers Give Their Views," *National Review,* July 1, 1996.
Joseph A. Califano	"Voters Bomboozled into Legalizing Drugs," *Human Events,* January 10, 1997. Available from 422 First St. SE, Washington, DC 20003.
Christian Science Monitor	"Legalization: No Answer," February 8, 1996.
Jeff Elliott	"Drug Prevention Placebo: How DARE Wastes Time, Money, and Police," *Reason,* March 1995.
Stephen Glass	"Don't You D.A.R.E.," *New Republic,* March 3, 1997.
Joe Hughes	"Doubts About DARE: Anti-Drug Program Criticized as Unproven," *San Diego Union-Tribune,* April 17, 1997. Available from PO Box 191, San Diego, CA 92119-4106.
Christina Kent	"Adolescent Drug Use Up," *American Medical News,* January 13, 1997. Available from American Medical Association, 535 N. Dearborn St., Chicago, IL 60610.
Gina Kolata	"Experts Are at Odds on How Best to Tackle Rise in Teen-Ager's Drug Use," *New York Times,* September 18, 1996.
Mike Males	"High on Lies: The Phony 'Teen Drug Crisis' Hides the Deadly Truths of the 'War on Drugs,'" *Extra,* September/October 1995.
Mike Males and Faye Docuyanan	"The Return of Reefer Madness," *Progressive,* May 1996.
Michael Massing	"Reefer Madness Strikes Again," *New York Times,* August 27, 1996.
Barry R. McCaffrey	"Prevention Programs Work," *Vital Speeches of the Day,* November 15, 1996.
John Mintz	"Getting a Financial High from Rope," *Washington Post National Weekly Edition,* January 13, 1997. Available from 1150 15th St. NW, Washington, DC 20071.
Ethan Nadelmann and Jennifer McNeely	"Doing Methadone Right," *Public Interest,* September 1996.
Mireya Navarro	"Marijuana Farms Are Flourishing Indoors, Producing a More Potent Drug," *New York Times,* November 24, 1996.
Charles O'Brien and Thomas McLellan	"Myths About the Treatment of Addiction," *Lancet,* January 27, 1996. Available from 245 West 17th St., New York, NY 10011.
William O'Brien, interview by George M. Anderson	"The Crisis in Drug Treatment," *America,* March 16, 1996.

George Soros	"Why the Drug War Cannot Be Won," *Washington Post National Weekly Edition,* February 10, 1997.
James A. Swartz, Arthur J. Lurigio, and Scott A. Slomka	"The Impact of IMPACT: An Assessment of the Effectiveness of a Jail-Based Treatment Program," *Crime & Delinquency,* October 1996. Available from 2455 Teller Road, Thousand Oaks, CA 91320.
Whitney A. Taylor	"Youth to Youth," *Drug Policy Letter,* Summer 1996. Available from 4455 Connecticut Ave. NW, Suite B-500, Washington, DC 20008-2302.
Andrew Peyton Thomas	"Marijuana and Mea Culpas," *American Enterprise,* May/June 1997. Available from PO Box 2013, Marion, OH 43305.
R. Emmett Tyrrell Jr.	"No to Drug Legalization," *American Spectator,* April 1996.
David Van Biema	"Just Say Life Skills," *Time,* November 11, 1996.
Mortimer B. Zuckerman	"Great Idea for Ruining Kids," *U.S. News & World Report,* February 24, 1997.

Organizations to Contact

The editors have compiled the following list of organizations concerned with the issues debated in this book. The descriptions are derived from materials provided by the organizations. All have publications or information available for interested readers. The list was compiled on the date of publication of the present volume; names, addresses, phone and fax numbers, and e-mail and Internet addresses may change. Be aware that many organizations take several weeks or longer to respond to inquiries, so allow as much time as possible.

American Council for Drug Education
136 E. 64th St.
New York, NY 10163
(800) 488-3784
(212) 758-8060
fax: (212) 758-6784
Internet: http://www.acde.org

The American Council for Drug Education informs the public about the harmful effects of abusing drugs and alcohol. It publishes educational materials, reviews, and scientific findings and develops educational media campaigns. The council's pamphlets, monographs, films, and other teaching aids address educators, parents, physicians, and employees.

Canadian Centre on Substance Abuse (CCSA)
75 Albert St., Suite 300
Ottawa, ON K1P 5E7
CANADA
(613) 235-4048
fax: (613) 235-8101

The CCSA works to minimize the harm associated with the use of alcohol, tobacco, and other drugs by sponsoring public debates on this issue. It disseminates information on the nature, extent, and consequences of substance abuse and supports organizations involved in substance abuse treatment, prevention, and educational programming. The center publishes the newsletter *Action News*.

Canadian Foundation for Drug Policy (CFDP)
70 MacDonald St.
Ottawa, ON K2P 1H6
CANADA
(613) 236-1027
fax: (613) 238-2891
e-mail: eoscapel@fox.nstn.ca
Internet: http://fox.nstn.ca/~eoscapel/cfdp/cfdp.html

Founded by several of Canada's leading drug policy specialists, the CFDP examines the objectives and consequences of Canada's drug laws and policies. When necessary, the foundation recommends alternatives that it believes would make Canada's drug policies more effective and humane. The CFDP discusses drug policy issues with the Canadian government, media, and general public. It also disseminates educational materials and maintains a website.

Cato Institute
1000 Massachusetts Ave. NW
Washington, DC 20001-5403
(202) 842-0200

The institute is a public policy research foundation dedicated to limiting the control of government and to protecting individual liberty. Cato, which strongly favors drug legalization, publishes the *Cato Journal* three times a year and the *Cato Policy Report* bimonthly.

Center on Addiction and Substance Abuse (CASA)
Columbia University
152 W. 57th St.
New York, NY 10019
(212) 841-5200
fax: (212) 956-8020
Internet: http://www.casacolumbia.org

CASA is a private, nonprofit organization that works to educate the public about the hazards of chemical dependency. The organization supports treatment as the best way to reduce chemical dependency. It produces publications describing the harmful effects of alcohol and drug addiction and effective ways to address the problem of substance abuse. It also distributes the monthly newsletter *START* and maintains a website.

Committees of Correspondence
11 John St., Room 506
New York, NY 10038
(212) 233-7151
fax: (212) 233-7063

The Committees of Correspondence is a national coalition of community groups that campaign against drug abuse among youth by publishing data about drugs and drug abuse. The coalition opposes drug legalization and advocates treatment for drug abusers. Its publications include the quarterly *Drug Abuse Newsletter,* the periodic *Drug Prevention Resource Manual,* and related pamphlets, brochures, and article reprints.

Drug Enforcement Administration (DEA)
700 Army Navy Dr.
Arlington, VA 22202
(202) 307-1000

The DEA is the federal agency charged with enforcing the nation's drug laws. The agency concentrates on stopping the smuggling and distribution of narcotics in the United States and abroad. It publishes the *Drug Enforcement Magazine* three times a year.

Drug Policy Foundation
4801 Massachusetts Ave. NW, #400
Washington, DC 20016
(202) 537-5005

The foundation supports legalizing many drugs and increasing the number of treatment programs for addicts. The foundation's publications include the bimonthly *Drug Policy Letter* and the book *The Great Drug War.* It also distributes *Press Clips,* an annual compilation of newspaper articles on drug legalization issues, as well as legislative updates.

Drugs Data Center and Clearinghouse
1600 Research Blvd.
Rockville, MD 20850
(800) 732-3277

The clearinghouse distributes the publications of the U.S. Department of Justice, the Drug Enforcement Administration, and other related federal agencies.

Hazelden Educational Materials
PO Box 176
Center City, MN 55012
(800) 328-9000
(612) 257-4010

Hazelden is a treatment center for alcoholism and drug addiction. Its Educational Materials division publishes and distributes a broad variety of materials on chemical dependency and recovery. A free catalog of these materials can be obtained by calling the toll-free number.

Heritage Foundation
214 Massachusetts Ave. NE
Washington, DC 20008-2302
(202) 546-4400

The Heritage Foundation is a conservative public policy research institute that opposes the legalization of drugs and advocates strengthening law enforcement to stop drug abuse. It publishes position papers on a broad range of topics, including drug issues. Its regular publications include the monthly *Policy Review,* the Backgrounder series of occasional papers, and the Heritage Lectures series.

Institute for a Drug-Free Workplace
1225 I St. NW, Suite 1000
Washington, DC 20005-3914
(202) 842-7400
fax: (202) 842-0022
Internet: http://www.drugfreeworkplace.org

The institute is dedicated to preserving the rights of employers and employees in substance-abuse prevention programs and to positively influencing the national debate on these issues. It publishes the *Guide to Dangerous Drugs,* the pamphlets *What Every Employee Should Know About Drug Abuse: Answers to 20 Good Questions* and *Does Drug Testing Work?* as well as several fact sheets.

Institute for Social Research
University of Michigan
426 Thompson
Ann Arbor, MI 48104-2321
(313) 747-4416
Internet: http://www.isr.umich.edu/

The institute conducts the annual Monitoring the Future Survey, which gathers data on drug use (including smoking) and attitudes toward drugs among eighth-, tenth-, and twelfth-grade students. Survey results are published by the National Institute on Drug Abuse.

International Narcotic Enforcement Officers Association (INEOA)
112 State St., Suite 1200
Albany, NY 12207
(518) 463-6232

The INEOA examines national and international narcotics laws and seeks ways to improve those laws and to prevent drug abuse. It also studies law enforcement methods to find the most effective ways to reduce illegal drug use. The association publishes a newsletter and the monthlies *International Drug Report* and *NarcOfficer.*

Libertarian Party
1528 Pennsylvania Ave. SE
Washington, DC 20003-3116
(202) 543-1988

The Libertarian Party is a political party whose goal is to protect individual rights and liberties. It advocates the repeal of all laws prohibiting the production, sale, possession, or use of drugs. The party believes law enforcement should focus on preventing violent crimes against persons and property rather than on prosecuting people who use drugs. It publishes the bimonthly *Libertarian Party News* and periodic *Issues Papers* and distributes a compilation of articles supporting drug legalization.

Lindesmith Center
c/o Ethan Nadelmann
888 Seventh Ave., Suite 2700
New York, NY 10106
fax: (212) 262-7580
e-mail: enadelmann@sorosny.org
Internet: http://www.lindesmith.org

The Lindesmith Center is a policy research institute that focuses on broadening the debate on drug policy and related issues. The center houses a library and information center; organizes seminars and conferences; acts as a link between scholars, government, and the media; directs a grant program in Europe; and undertakes projects on special topics such as methadone policy reform and alternatives to drug testing in the workplace. It addresses issues of drug policy reform through a variety of projects, including the Drug Policy Seminar series, the International Harm Reduction Development Program, and the Methadone Policy Reform Project. The center publishes fact sheets on topics such as needle and syringe availability, drug prohibition and the U.S. prison system, and drug education.

Narcotic Educational Foundation of America (NEFA)
5055 Sunset Blvd.
Los Angeles, CA 90027
(213) 663-5171

The NEFA provides educational materials on the dangers of drug use and abuse. It maintains a library specializing in drug abuse topics, and its publications include *Get the Answers—an Open Letter to Youth* and *Some Things You Should Know About Prescription Drugs.*

Pg 16

* 9 — 12 yrs old are using drugs
and more are growing increasingly
tolerant toward drug use.

* Significant erosions in Anti-drug
attitudes and more 9 to 12 yrs old using
illicit drugs, particularly marijuana

* 4th, 5th + 6th graders are less likely
to think drugs are harmful.

Pg 17   Susceptibility to Drug Abuse Incr.

one in four children was offered drugs
during 1996. white children report ---

See Table 2

New Friends and Pressures
* Junior High and High School
Pg 21 Ominous statistic

Narcotics Anonymous (NA)
PO Box 9999
Van Nuys, CA 91409
(818) 780-3951

NA, comprising more than eighteen thousand groups worldwide, is an organization of recovering drug addicts who meet regularly to help each other abstain from drugs. It publishes the monthlies *NA Way Magazine* and *Newsline.*

National Acupuncture Detoxification Association (NADA)
PO Box 1927
Vancouver, WA 98668-1927
(206) 254-0186

NADA promotes acupuncture as a treatment for drug addiction. It favors government-funded drug treatment programs and opposes drug legalization. NADA publishes the *NADA Newsletter* annually.

National Clearinghouse for Alcohol and Drug Information (NCADI)
PO Box 2345
Rockville, MD 20847-2345
(800) 729-6686
Internet: http://www.health.org

The clearinghouse distributes publications of the U.S. Department of Health and Human Services, the National Institute on Drug Abuse, and other federal agencies concerned with alcohol and drug abuse, including the *Substance Abuse Resource Guides* and the newsletter *Prevention Pipeline.*

National Council on Alcoholism and Drug Dependence (NCADD)
12 W. 21st St., 7th Fl.
New York, NY 10010
(800) 622-2255
(212) 206-6770
fax: (212) 645-1690

The National Council on Alcoholism and Drug Dependence works to educate Americans about alcohol and drug abuse. It provides community-based prevention and education programs as well as information and service referrals. The NCADD publishes pamphlets, fact sheets, and other materials that provide statistics on chemical dependency.

National Council on Patient Information and Education
666 Eleventh St. NW, Suite 810
Washington, DC 20001
(202) 347-6711

The council consists of pharmaceutical manufacturers, health care professional organizations, and consumer groups. It provides information on the issue of prescription drugs and calls for increased discussion between doctors and patients regarding prescribed drugs. It publishes the *Directory of Prescription Drug Information and Education Programs and Resources.*

National Institute on Drug Abuse (NIDA)
U.S. Department of Health and Human Services
5600 Fishers Ln.
Rockville, MD 20857
(301) 443-6245
Internet: http://www.nida.nih.gov

The NIDA supports and conducts research on drug abuse—including the yearly Monitoring the Future Survey—in order to improve addiction prevention, treatment, and policy efforts. It publishes the bimonthly *NIDA Notes* newsletter, the periodic *NIDA Capsules* fact sheets, and a catalog of research reports and public education materials such as *Marijuana: Facts for Teens.*

National Organization for the Reform of Marijuana Laws (NORML)
2001 S St. NW, Suite 640
Washington, DC 20009
(202) 483-5500

NORML fights to legalize marijuana and to help those who have been convicted and sentenced for possessing or selling marijuana. In addition to pamphlets and position papers, it publishes the newsletter *Marijuana Highpoints* and the quarterly *NORML's Active Resistance.*

Office of National Drug Control Policy
Executive Office of the President
Drugs and Crime Clearinghouse
PO Box 6000
Rockville, MD 20849-6000

The Office of National Drug Control Policy is responsible for formulating the government's national drug strategy and the president's antidrug policy as well as coordinating the federal agencies responsible for stopping drug trafficking. Drug policy studies are available upon request.

RAND Corporation
Distribution Services
1700 Main St.
PO Box 2138
Santa Monica, CA 90407-2138
(310) 393-0411, ext. 6686

The RAND Corporation is a research institution that seeks to improve public policy through research and analysis. RAND's Drug Policy Research Center publishes information on the costs, prevention, and treatment of alcohol and drug abuse as well as on trends in drug-law enforcement. Its extensive list of publications includes the book *Sealing the Borders,* by Peter Reuter.

Reason Foundation
3451 S. Sepulveda Blvd., Suite 400
Los Angeles, CA 90034
(310) 391-2245

This public policy organization researches contemporary social and political problems and promotes libertarian philosophy and free-market principles. It publishes the monthly *Reason* magazine, which contains articles and editorials critical of the war on drugs and smoking regulation.

Wisconsin Clearinghouse for Prevention Resources
1552 University Ave.
Madison, WI 53705
(800) 322-1468
fax: (608) 262-6346
Internet: http://www.uhs.wisc.edu/wch/

The clearinghouse produces and distributes prevention materials for schools, communities, colleges and universities, prevention agencies, and health care organizations. It offers books, videos, posters, pamphlets, and software on a wide variety of prevention topics, including alcohol and other drug abuse, violence prevention and anger management, conflict resolution, self-esteem enhancement, teen pregnancy, and sexually transmitted diseases.

Index

Index

Index